the web designer's 101 most important decisions

the web designer's 101 most important decisions

Professional secrets for a winning website

Scott Parker

ILEX

Contents

THE WEB DESIGNER'S
101 MOST IMPORTANT DECISIONS

First published in the United Kingdom in 2012 by
ILEX
210 High Street
Lewes
East Sussex
BN7 2NS

Copyright © 2012 The Ilex Press Limited

Publisher: Alastair Campbell
Creative Director: James Hollywell
Managing Editor: Nick Jones
Senior Editor: Ellie Wilson
Commissioning Editor: Emma Shackleton
Art Director: Julie Weir
Designer: Richard Wolfströme

British Library Cataloguing-in-Publication Data
A catalogue record for this book is available
from the British Library.

ISBN: 978-1-908150-25-7

Printed and bound in China

Colour Origination by Ivy Press Reprographics

10 9 8 7 6 5 4 3 2 1

Introduction

Embarking on any web project can be a daunting prospect, and it can be difficult to know where to begin. What does your website need? How will you build it? What is it going to look like? How will anyone ever find it?

This book takes a look at all the things you need to consider when building a website and offers advice on how you can achieve your goals. It gives examples of good practice and provides details of useful sites and services to help you on your way, but most importantly it will highlight all the key decisions you will have to make. It's not so much about telling you what to do, but more what you need to think about if you want to be sure of success.

Although much of this book is aimed at budding web designers looking to build their first website, it is also helpful for those not wanting to get their hands dirty. If you are commissioning someone else to do the work, having a basic understanding of the technologies and the principles of web design will make it a lot easier to create an effective brief and understand what it is that your website needs. And even professionals need a helping hand from time to time. This book offers a useful checklist to make sure they have covered all the bases.

What this book also shows is that you don't have to be a coding expert to get a fantastic website. There is almost always a quick and easy way to get what you need, with someone else doing all the hard work for you. This isn't a cop-out either—no matter how good you are, it often makes perfect sense to take a few short-cuts if you want to save time, money, and your sanity.

We only skim the surface of what could be written about the design and development of websites—many sections could easily have had whole chapters devoted to them, some whole books—but we highlight all the issues you should explore. The web is full of great advice, but sometimes you need a nudge in the right direction, and this book gives you a starting point to find out more.

Of course, any book on web design can only provide a snapshot of the time. Things move quickly on the web and what might be accepted as best practice now could be considered outdated before you know it. But however much the web changes, the principles of good web design will not. As the trends, opinions, and technology evolve, the issues raised in this book will largely remain the same. If you plan properly, focus on providing content that people want, and make it all as accessible and easy to use as possible, then you will be well on your way to building a winning website.

About Scott Parker

Scott Parker has been working with the web almost since it began, seeing it from all sides—as client, supplier, and commentator. Over the years he has worked with specialists in pretty much every field on a diverse range of projects, giving him a valuable insight into what works and what doesn't.

He helped build one of the UK Government's first websites in 1994, and went on to manage one of the UK's first profit-making online news services. Scott was also Associate Editor of *Internet Magazine*, the UK's leading internet title during the dotcom boom and bust, where he wrote extensively on how to build and manage great websites.

Until the end of 2009 Scott was Head of Product Design for a leading health information company. This involved building complex web-based applications for clients such as the Department of Health and the NHS and various consumer-facing health websites, often working in partnership with major online publishers such as *Telegraph.co.uk*, *Saga*, *netdoctor.co.uk*, *Channel4.com*, and *Times Online*.

He now runs his own consultancy business, working on all sorts of web projects, from designing simple websites for small businesses to developing complex database-driven applications.

He's always happy to offer advice, so drop him a line at scott@scottparker.co.uk if you have any questions.

Chapter 1
Before You Begin

Why do you need a website?

So you have decided that you need a website, and you are probably right, but do you know *why* you need a website? Do you know exactly what you want from it? It's an important question, but it is surprising how often people don't think about what they really expect from having an online presence.

There are many reasons why any organization or business needs a website, of course. Almost all of us will turn to the web before purchasing a product or service, even if we are just looking for a real-world place to buy it from. If you do not have a web presence, you could lose business—but if your website is better than your competitors, it could give you the edge.

A website can be an effective marketing tool and going online will give you a much wider reach than any brick-and-mortar store or advertising campaign—you can turn a local business into an international one without even having to leave the house.

The web can save you money. It allows you to automate many processes that would normally take up valuable time, like taking orders or requests for information. It lets you communicate quickly and easily with your customers, providing what they need without them having to give you a call or come into your store.

It also allows you to distribute content that would otherwise be very expensive to deliver, including audio and video. If you're selling digital content that people are prepared to pay for, the margins can be huge, as the costs might well be same if you provide it to ten people or 10,000.

You need consider how much time and money you are expecting to spend on your website, and how long it might take to see a return on that investment. How many extra sales would you need to pay for the development? How many more people will see what you are offering? Will it all be worth the effort?

It's not all about the money, of course. You might simply want to entertain, inform, or provide assistance without an eye on the profits, and the web will let you reach as wide an audience as you can without the need for bags of cash. Just be clear about why you are building your website and think about what others would like to get from it.

Whatever your goals, be realistic about what you can expect from the web. It will not be a miracle cure, so don't expect thousands of people to come flocking to your site as soon as it is launched. Building the site is only half the job, and you have to actively maintain and promote the site if it is going attract visitors. It's not easy to build an effective online presence, but if you are prepared to put in the time and energy the rewards can be great.

Do it yourself?

If you have decided to do it yourself but are not a hardcore web developer, you can make things a little easier by using a content management system like WordPress. It will still require a lot of work to build the website of your dreams, but you might not need to get your hands dirty with the code.

There is a huge amount of support out there to get you started, for example, www.wpbeginner.com.

Building a website on your own can seem like an attractive prospect. You don't have to pay anyone else for a start, but you also know you have complete control over it. On the other hand, it is rarely a painless process and getting it wrong could be embarrassing, or worse.

Before embarking on a web project, be sure you have all the knowledge and expertise necessary to succeed. Although the basics of HTML and CSS are pretty simple to pick up, things can soon get tricky when you look to add dynamic elements or databases. Graphic design, copywriting, and marketing are also essential elements of any web project and take much time and effort to get right. Anyone can make a website, but not so many people can make one that works well in all areas.

If you are an amateur web designer or complete novice, think twice before setting off alone on a website that affects your livelihood. If you run a business that you think really needs an online presence, it is much better to pay a professional to help you realize exactly what you want.

The trouble is, where do you start? There are thousands of suppliers out there with very differing degrees of size, quality, and cost.

You might get quotes varying from $100 to $10,000 for exactly the same piece of work, so you need to be realistic about what you can expect for the price you are prepared to pay. Larger agencies charging at the higher end should do a professional job, but they might not always be so flexible. One-man bands doing it for pocket money in their spare time might not have the capacity or expertise to give you all you need.

It's always best to act on a recommendation, if you can, but sound out a few possible suppliers and try to talk to someone face-to-face or over the phone to get a feel for whether they are someone you can work with. Look at their portfolios to see what they have done before and see if it fits with what you are trying to do.

Whether you are doing it all yourself or bringing people in, you still need to think about all the elements covered in this book before you get started on your web project. If you do the research, plan it out, and decide what you need before you start, everything will go far more smoothly.

Research and feedback

EVERNOTE   LEARN MORE | NOTEWORTHY BLOG | THE TRUNK

Make a note. Or 500,000 of them.

Evernote makes it easy to remember things big and small from your notable life using your computer, phone, and the web. Get started today with a free account.

1. Capture everything.

Chances are, if you can see it or think of it, Evernote can help you remember it. Type a text note. Clip a web page. Snap a photo. Grab a screenshot. Evernote will keep it all safe.

2. Organize it. (Or let us do it.)

Everything you capture is automatically processed, indexed, and made searchable. If you like, you can add tags or organize notes into different notebooks.

Even if you have a very clear idea about what you want from your website, it is important to get other people's views and find out what else is out there. You won't have thought of everything, so a bit of research will help make sure you know exactly what is needed.

Make sure you know your audience and what they are looking for. If your business is already up and running, ask your customers what they think. These are the people you are looking to impress, after all, so if you can cater for their needs then you are on to a winner.

If you already have a website that you are looking to redevelop, consider what works and what doesn't. Take a look at the traffic stats to see what are the most popular pages and those that everyone ignores, but bear in mind that people might not be looking at some content because they can't find it, not because they are not interested.

Organize some user-testing, where you can observe exactly how people are navigating your site. Getting this done properly with specialists using eye-tracking technology and specially selected user-types can be very expensive, so if you have limited resources just get friends or relatives who are not too familiar with your site to give you some feedback. Tell them not to be too kind though; the negative comments are usually far more useful than the positive ones.

Check out the competition and steal all their best ideas. You'll have to stop short of completely ripping them off, of course, but there is nothing wrong with building the sensible features they have into your website. You'll also want to differentiate your site from everyone else's, so also look for things that your rivals haven't done.

If you are not quite sure who your competition is, Google the keywords that best describe what you are offering and see what comes up. If you get few results, it could mean that you have found a gap in the market—either that, or nobody is interested in what you are offering!

Look beyond your competitors to find sites that you think look good and work well—follow web design blogs like www.alistapart.com or check out sites nominated for accolades like the Webby Awards: www.webbyawards.com. It's also well worth reading books that cover these areas.

A good way to record and organize the things you like and the ideas you have is to use an online tool like Evernote. You can capture anything, like a screenshot, a bit of text, a photo, or even a voice recording, and add it to your notebook wherever you are using browser tools and mobile apps. You can then easily access your "notes" and organize them to help you write your website specification. Find out more at www.evernote.com.

Alexa (www.alexa.com) can be a useful tool to assess the competition and follow the latest trends. Data will be limited for all but the largest sites, but it can still help you identify your audience and the kinds of things they are looking at.

Planning for success

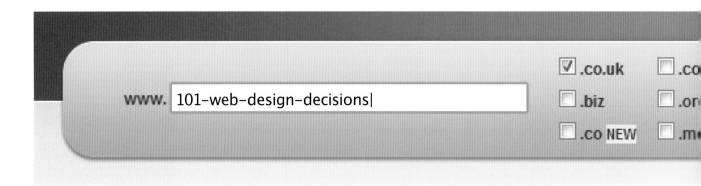

It's very easy to get overexcited about a new website and run headlong into building a masterpiece, but once you have established that going online is something you really must do, you have to plan carefully to make sure you get exactly what you need.

Whether you are building a site yourself or recruiting someone to do it for you, you should write a clear specification that includes all the functionality you might require. This doesn't have to be particularly detailed—in fact, bullet points often work better than long explanations—but it needs to cover areas like structure, content, design, and functionality. Don't forget to consider how you will maintain and promote your site after it has launched, too.

If you are writing a brief for a web designer, allow them enough freedom to suggest their own ideas on how things should be done. Don't detail how every element should look and work—even if you think you know exactly what you want, remember that they are the experts when it comes to building websites and this is why you are paying them.

Create a draft sitemap, identifying all the pages you think you'll need and how you think they should be grouped. A picture paints a thousand words, so a rough sketch of how you think the key pages should look can be useful. It doesn't have to be artistic, it just needs to highlight the main elements required. Links to other sites that you like are also helpful.

Start writing draft content as early as possible—it is much easier to build a site around content that is already there. The same goes for the branding: sorting out your logo and preferred color scheme will help direct how the site should be designed.

Ensure that you have all the tools and resources you need in place and think about the schedule. It's no good looking at a launch date a few weeks in the future if you are not going to have everything ready in time. Set targets for each key milestone, such as signing off the design, completing the structure, finalizing the content, and starting user-testing.

A plan makes sure all those involved know what is expected of them and when, so everybody is less likely to be hit with nasty surprises further down the line. The plan should be flexible, of course, but the more you think about what needs to be done before you begin the more likely your site will be a success.

Providers like 1and1.co.uk make it extremely cheap and easy to register your domain name.

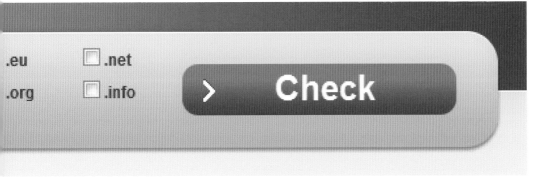

.eu   ☐ .net

.org   ☐ .info

> **Check**

If you haven't registered a domain name for your site, you'll have to look around to see what is available. You should consider these points:

• A .com extension is the most sought after, but that means it is often extremely difficult to get the domain you want. Don't go for a hard-to-remember name just to get the extension.

• Look to get a domain with the relevant country code, like co.uk in the UK, and extensions that are targeted at your sector, like .org or org.uk domains for charities.

• Consider what sites have similar domain names or have the same name with a different extension. It can create confusion—and even embarrassment—if someone mistakes another site for yours.

• Don't go crazy buying up every variation of a domain that you can, unless you are trying to protect a brand name. You should only ever use and promote one domain name, even if you register more.

• Take care going for the less common domain types, because people aren't quite so familiar with them. If you pick something like mydomain.me.uk, some people will inevitably misread this and go to mydomain.co.uk instead, and if that is a competitor you might lose business.

• Only buy domains from reputable companies and never by phone or post. There are plenty of people trying to scam you out of money for domains you don't need.

Chapter 2
Technologies

The web-design challenge

You don't need huge technical expertise to create a website, but it certainly helps if you understand a bit about the key technologies required and how they should be used.

You have various choices on what road to go down, like which scripting language you opt for and what software you use. There is no right or wrong route to take—it will depend on what you are trying to achieve and what resources you have to hand. You just need to remember that the technology doesn't really matter to the user; they won't care if a video is shown with HTML5 or Flash as long as they get to see it without any problems.

Your aim should always be to create a website that works for everyone who views it, whatever it looks like under the hood. That can be a challenge because different people will use different web browsers and some will have versions that do not support all the technologies you might want to employ. Your site will be viewed on mobile devices and screens with many different resolutions, and you should also remember that not everybody has perfect vision. Catering for everybody is not always straightforward.

You will be on the right track if your code is well structured and follows the recognized standards, but you will always need to provide fallbacks for those that don't have the necessary software installed.

How your page looks is important, but remember that people are coming to your site for the content. It's fine if some people miss out on the design features that are only supported by the latest browsers, but you should never exclude anybody from seeing what your website has to say.

The code

HTML, or Hypertext Markup Language, forms the main building blocks of almost every web page. It has been around since before the World Wide Web was born and has changed remarkably little over the last twenty years. The basics of HTML are easy to learn, so even if you are not building a website yourself it is worth becoming familiar with the key elements, like how to create links, embed images, or format text.

However using HTML alone will only allow you to create "static" websites. Most websites now have dynamic web pages that change every time they are loaded. These are usually driven by a database and need a server-side scripting language.

PHP is probably the most widely used scripting language and is usually used with a MySQL database. Both are free and can be installed on almost any platform, although it is more often associated with Linux.

Microsoft's Active Server Pages (ASP) is the main competitor, although now succeeded by the ASP.NET web application framework. This needs a Windows server and a Microsoft SQL database.

It is hard to say which is better, as it will depend on the project, but PHP developers are usually cheaper and easier to come by. ASP.NET might be more suitable for complex web applications that need a large database.

There are plenty of other alternatives, such as Java, Ruby on Rails, and Coldfusion, but none have quite the same level of adoption and support. The danger is that further down the line you might struggle to find the expertise you need to carry out further developments.

If you need a bit of tutoring, there is plenty of assistance online. A good place to get started is www.w3schools.com.

Using style sheets

The Web Designer Wall (http://webdesigneArwall.com) is a great resource for ideas, helpful tutorials, and information, such as this post on CSS fixes.

CSS code allows you to set rules for the design and layout of your website that can be applied to every page.

Although you'll use HTML to build the overall structure of your web pages, the design and layout should be controlled by Cascading Style Sheets (CSS). This allows you to separate content from presentation, so you can change the way your site looks without having to change the way it works.

Before CSS came along, presentational attributes of web pages were defined in the HTML—you couldn't just say "all headers should be blue" or "all paragraphs should be in Arial font," you had to repeat the relevant HTML many times on every page.

CSS allows you to set rules that can be applied to any element on the page. The rules lower down take precedence over the rules above, hence the "cascade." CSS is usually used alongside the HTML <div> tag, which defines a section or group of elements to create a layout for a web page. So you could create <div> tags for the navigation, main content, and sub-content, and use the CSS to put the navigation across the top of the page and the content divided into two columns.

Although styles can be contained within the code of a web page, even applied to specific elements, it is much better to put all the required styles in a single file—the style sheet—which can then be called on by every page. This means you only have to change the CSS in one file to change the way all your web pages look. This makes life much easier when you want to make changes, but also helps ensure that the design is consistent across your whole site.

You can create style sheets for different needs, such as for displaying your site on mobile platforms or for printing out web pages. You can even let your users select the style sheet they want to use to display your site, which can be particularly useful for people with visual impairments.

Despite the considerable benefits of CSS, adoption has been remarkably slow. Different browsers have interpreted CSS in different ways, meaning designers have had to learn a variety of methods to get their pages to look the same for everybody.

CSS is easy to pick up, but knowing all the fixes that might be required takes years of experience. Luckily, there are always people out there that are willing to share their wisdom.

Sticking to standards

Standards are important! If everyone accepted and followed web standards, it'd be cheaper and easier to develop websites that are accessible to everyone, on all kinds of devices, now and in the future. It sounds like common sense, but unfortunately not everyone has been singing from the same hymn sheet.

Browser manufacturers have finally got their act together and are now "standards-compliant," but some browsers can still be quite forgiving and will display your website properly even if there are a few errors in the code. This might sound helpful, but the problem is that some developers might be less inclined to follow the standards if they don't have to.

You need to consider how your site will look for all potential users—will it work on a mobile platform? What happens when a new browser version is launched? How will someone with visual impairment see your site? If your code

sticks to the standards, then you can be more confident that your pages will work as you intend wherever they are seen.

The principle web standards are set by the World Wide Web Consortium: www.w3.org. HTML 4.01 is the latest agreed standard for HTML, although it has been succeeded by XHTML 1.0.

XHTML, or extensible Hypertext Markup Language, looks and works much the same as HTML but is based on XML. It has stricter rules, but using XHTML will mean your site is more likely to work across all devices and will continue to do so. You can convert your HTML code to XHTML with a free tool at sourceforge.net/projects/tidy, but it is better to start with XHTML in the first place.

The latest recommended standard for Cascading Style Sheets is CSS2.1. Although

HTML validator icon

it was a long road to finally getting it agreed in 2011, progress on CSS3 modules has been much quicker.

You can check your HTML and XHTML using the W3C Markup Validation Sevice at validator.w3.org and CSS at jigsaw.w3.org/css-validator. The W3C also provides a unified validator called Unicorn that will check a variety of other standards (validator.w3.org/unicorn). Other validation tools and browser plug-ins are also available—like HTML Validator for Firefox—and validation is often built into editing suites like Dreamweaver.

The arrival of HTML5 on the scene presents web developers with a bit of a dilemma because it has yet to achieve a full recommendation from W3C. This means you might find that your validator shows errors in your code if you add HTML5 elements. You may be able to set your validator to check HTML5 code, but the results could be unreliable as the standards are subject to change, and it might not flag up the errors that would fail the strict XHTML validation.

W3C® Markup Validation Service
Check the markup (HTML, XHTML, ...) of Web documents

Jump To: Congratulations · Icons

This document was successfully checked as XHTML + RDFa!

Result:	Passed
Address :	http://www.bbc.co.uk/
Encoding :	utf-8 (detect automatically)
Doctype :	XHTML + RDFa (detect automatically)
Root Element:	html
Root Namespace:	http://www.w3.org/1999/xhtml

I ♥ VALIDATOR

The W3C validators rely on community support for hosting and development. **Donate** and help us build better tools for a better web.   2343   Flattr

W3C validator

Keeping it clean

This BBC website is a good example of a well-structured page, as can be seen using the W3C's semantic extractor tool: www.w3.org/2003/12/semantic-extractor.html.

Most of the people that visit your site won't be interested in the slightest in how your code looks, but that doesn't mean it shouldn't be clean and tidy. Following the standards is a good place to start, but the structure of the code and how the elements are named is also important.

HTML should be written semantically, which means that it should only be used to describe the meaning of information in a web page rather than how it looks. Content should be separated from presentation, which would be handled by the CSS in an external style sheet. This will make your website more efficient and quicker to load.

Although it is still possible to control some presentational aspects with HTML, it should be avoided. For instance, the <i> tag can be used to make text italic, but the better option is to use <em> to denote emphasis and then use CSS to specify how you want that to be presented.

The structure of your web page should be clear and logical. It will have a <head> first that includes information about your page including the <title>, then within the <body>, the most important heading on the page should have an <h1> tag, the subheading <h2>, and headings below that <h3>. Paragraphs should be marked up as paragraphs, lists as lists, and so on. Images should be given title attributes that describe what they are. The navigation should be marked up as a list of links and then styled accordingly, making it much easier to add and remove items or change how it looks.

Your content will be wrapped in <div> elements that are given an id or class that should describe their content or function, not their appearance, such as <div id="navigation"> or <div class="news-item">. All these elements should follow a logical hierarchy, such as: Header > Main navigation > Sub-navigation > Content > Other information > Footer. HTML5 takes this principle further by introducing new elements for the main blocks of a website like <header>, <nav>, <footer>, and <section>.

If you take a look at your code it should be clear what information is on the page and what content is the most important without needing to see what is actually displayed. Remember that not all visitors to your site will be looking at your wonderful design—search engine spiders are only interested in your content, and if your code is uncluttered, written semantically, and well structured, then your site will fare much better in the rankings.

Making your code easier to read also means it will be far easier for you—or anyone else—to make changes. You can also add comments to your code to describe more clearly what each part does. These are not shown to the user but can be very helpful when developing a more complex page, particularly if you are using a dynamic scripting language. Comments can also be added to any CSS or JavaScript files to help make them easier to manage.

Cross-browser compatibility

You'd have thought that a clear set of web standards would mean that all web browsers would follow them in the same way, but sadly that it is not the case. It was not so long ago that the main browser manufacturers pretty much ignored the standards and introduced their own proprietary code, but the situation has thankfully become much better in recent years.

The latest versions of the main browsers—Microsoft Internet Explorer, Mozilla Firefox, Google Chrome, Apple Safari, and Opera—follow the W3C standards. This means that if you write standards-compliant code, all should look rosy whatever browser your site is seen on. Or maybe not. There are often still minor differences between browsers, and things have been further complicated by the development of new standards like HTML5 and CSS3. New browser versions are now coming out almost every month.

Not everyone has the latest versions though, and you need to consider what your site looks like for all users. You should have all the main browsers installed so that you can test them, but you won't be able to have every version. That's where you need services like Adobe BrowserLab (browserlab.adobe.com), which previews your web content across all browsers and platforms and advises what might need changing. It's free until April 2012, but Adobe might start charging from then, so you could try browsershots.org, a free alternative.

Most browsers have their issues, but Internet Explorer 6 in particular has been the bane of web developers for long time. Despite being over ten years old and superseded by several newer versions, IE6 still has a small but significant share of the browser market. Microsoft is trying its best to get everyone upgraded, but it is still the browser that refuses to die.

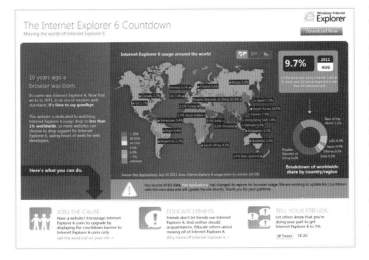

The problem with IE6 is that is does not support web standards and your pages could look quite different to what you intend. It is also unstable and has many security vulnerabilities, so many large companies have withdrawn all support for this ancient browser. If you are one of those still using it, please upgrade now!

So, should you bother with IE6? It partly depends on your audience: if you know that a reasonably large proportion of your users are still stuck in the dark ages, it might be worth at least making sure your site works for these people even it doesn't look perfect. Some IE fixes are fairly standard and easy to implement—some are even required for later versions—so it is worth applying those where necessary, but don't blow a blood vessel trying to make it look perfect.

011

HTML5 and the future

Good old HTML4 has been around since 1997 and has not been updated since 2000. It has served us well, but it is by no means perfect. It has been joined by XHTML and various other specifications to help form the basis of most of the web pages we see today, but it does not really satisfy the needs of many modern websites, particularly around the support for multimedia content.

HTML5 attempts to define a single markup language for the web and introduce powerful and flexible features that help create complex web applications and content more efficiently. It started life in 2007, but it's only relatively recently that web designers have really been taking it seriously. It is still in development and probably won't get the full W3C recommendation until 2014, but it is now at the stage where most of the main features are well defined and supported by the latest web browsers.

The key new features are the <video>, <audio>, and <canvas> elements, making it much easier to include and control multimedia and graphic content, as well as introducing elements to improve the semantic structure of a web page.

Along with HTML5, we are also seeing the development of CSS3 modules to give you more power over your layouts. Support is still patchy, but check out css3generator.com to demonstrate some of the new elements and get the necessary code.

Although all the latest browsers support HTML5 and CSS3, it is not always consistent so you'll still need to do those cross-browser checks. Unfortunately there will still be those who haven't upgraded their browsers for years, so you'll need to detect support for any HTML5 features you adopt and provide fallbacks as necessary. Perhaps one day everyone on the web will be able to sample the joys of HTML5—but maybe we will need HTML6 by then.

So what can you do with HTML5 and other new technologies? The Big Three are keen to showcase the capabilities of their latest browsers. Watch their demos at:

www.chromeexperiments.com
www.apple.com/html5
ie.microsoft.com/testdrive

Using JavaScript

JQuery takes the pain out of using JavaScript and there are plenty of resources to show you how to get impressive dynamic effects on your site.

Features like date selection are made easy using the YUI framework at yuilibrary.com

JavaScript is a powerful scripting language commonly used to create the dynamic, interactive elements of web pages. It can run in the browser, responding to user actions immediately rather than going back to the server. Popular uses are for image rollovers, creating popup windows, and validating forms, but it can do so much more.

Becoming a JavaScript pro takes much time and some skill, but thankfully there are libraries available that greatly simplify JavaScript programming so that even a novice can get to grips with it quite quickly.

JQuery is the most popular JavaScript library and is used by a huge proportion of the websites you see today. It is free, open-source software and lets developers create impressive effects and animations, dynamic forms, tables, and much more.

You don't even have to worry about writing all the code yourself—a wide variety of plug-ins is available for you to implement on your pages with very little effort. There are thousands of people developing plug-ins for jQuery, which they share with the community. Not all of them are perfect, but it doesn't take long to find the most popular and reliable examples.

JQuery also provides a user-interface library that has been built on top of the JavaScript library. This offers a selection of the most common effects and widgets used to build interactive websites.

You can add complex behaviors like drag-and-drop or resizing and sorting tables; features like autocomplete on forms, date pickers, and tabs; and animated transitions. Although jQuery is *de rigueur* these days, there are alternatives. Mootools and Prototype

are other widely used JavaScript frameworks, and the YUI Library on the Yahoo Developer Network provides a variety of utilities and controls for building web frontends.

More than 99% of all web users will have JavaScript enabled on their web browser, but not quite everybody. You should make sure that your site works with JavaScript switched off, providing alternative content as necessary.

This is harder to achieve for more complex web-based applications, but at the very least users should be presented with an explanation of why JavaScript is required rather than giving them a broken page.

Using Flash

Flash is an extremely powerful multimedia platform used to create interactive web pages. It is often used for animations and the delivery of audio and video content, but you can find all sorts of sites and applications entirely driven by Flash.

It has been around since the early days of the web but is now owned and developed by Adobe. Although you need a browser plug-in to view Flash content, the vast majority of web users will have it installed.

You'll need software to develop Flash content, and Adobe's Flash Professional package is not cheap. However, there are more affordable alternatives—such as SWiSH Max (www.swishzone.com) and KoolMoves (www.koolmoves.com)—and there are a variety of utilities that will produce specific features like banner adverts or photo galleries in Flash.

Over the years Flash has faced criticism on a number of issues, but many of the perceived flaws have now diminished. One claim is that Flash is bad for search engine optimization, but Google has indexed Flash sites without trouble for some time. Some people also have accessibility concerns, but Adobe has worked hard to provide tools to help make sure Flash content is accessible to all. As with all web design, you just need to think beyond the aesthetics and consider all the necessary requirements for your site.

Flash has been hugely successful at creating rich web content, but the future may not be quite so bright. Apple gave Adobe a body blow when it decided not to provide Flash support on the iPhone or iPad but to embrace HTML5 instead. Websites were therefore forced to look at the alternatives to delivering their multimedia content.

Below: SWISH Max (www.swishzone.com). Bottom: Flex is a powerful open-sourced framework based on Flash, used for developing complex web-based, mobile, and desktop applications. It's particularly good for data visualization, like the online trading platform provided at www.trademonster.com.

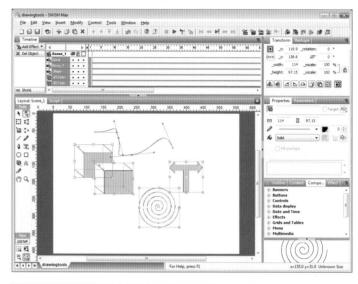

HTML5 vs Flash Showcase

The Apple HTML5 demos left party arts work with Safari (4.7% of all users on all devices). Some HTML5 features work, others won't work on other browsers. As a matter of fact, HTML5 is not really a standard at all. The Flash TODAY demos might portray show how 97% of all websites can experience Flash the way it is supposed to be today & tomorrow. Tech & innovation By the way, these Flash examples are extremely hard or simply impossible to build with HTML5.

Developers & users like to choose

HTML5 compared to Flash is like a hot compared to an umbrella. Then can be used together, but a hot won't replace an umbrella.
In May 2010, 8.67% of all online users are on iPhone or iPad (HTML).
In May 2010, 97.00% of all online users have the Flash Player 10 installed.
In May 2010, 97.00% of all online users CAN'T see HTML5 video h.264.
These speedtest you'd Flash Player 10.1 outperform HTML5 canvas.
With these figures in mind, don't it make sense to learn Flash and jump back in time with HTML5?

Go to FlashLab (www.flashlab.com) to see how HTML5 squares up to the old timer. Hint: FlashLab points out that HTML5 still has some catching up to do.

"We Choose the Moon" recreates the Apollo 11 lunar mission and is a great example of the joys of Flash: www.wechoosethemoon.org.

Not so long ago, Flash was by far the most common way to provide audio and video, but the rise of HTML5 means that it is often only provided as a fallback for those with older browsers. The new <canvas> element used with WebGL is also starting to become more popular, and even the likes of jQuery is being used for animated effects that were once only possible with Flash.

One of the most popular uses for Flash is for advertising, but the problem is that not everyone likes adverts on their web pages and will do all that they can to block them. This has led to the development of Flash-blocking plug-ins for all the major browsers, preventing all Flash from loading unless you specifically allow it.

Flash isn't dead yet, however. HTML5 still has to really prove its worth, become more efficient, and gain more support before it can take over. Flash has been used to create some great websites over many years, and there are still plenty of areas where it really is the only practical solution. (See www.flashlab.com, which compares Flash favorably.)

So is it wise to use Flash? The answer depends on what you are doing. If the things you are looking to do can be more easily achieved using CSS and jQuery, like navigation buttons and transitions, then you don't need Flash. And how much do you care about Apple users? Will your site still work for those people, even if they don't see your site in its full glory?

The real problem is that Flash development can be expensive. If you have the tools and skills you need already, then great. If not, you might find that recruiting someone who does—and going back to them each time you need to make a change—might bust your budget.

Using a content management system

WordPress's editing interface is pretty straighforward and allows you to preview how your web page will look before publishing.

Drupal is the largest competitor to WordPress and works in a similar way. Older versions required a bit more thought to use and manage, but the latest interface is more akin to WordPress: Drupal.org.

Building a website is one thing, but maintaining it can be an even greater challenge. If you have news and information that is changing regularly, updating the code manually and uploading it every time can soon become a chore. This is where content management systems save the day, making it simple to make changes and add content to your web pages with nothing more than a web browser.

Even small sites can benefit from content management systems because you can give anyone access to update the site wherever they might be, and they don't even need to have any technical skills.

Although you could build your own content management system, there are plenty of extremely capable packages available that can make creating and maintaining a website easy.

The most popular is WordPress, which is open-source software built by a huge community of volunteers. It is incredibly easy to get started; you just download the latest version and upload to your own webspace. WordPress boasts that the installation can be completed in just five minutes.

Once set up, you can do pretty much everything you need to update your site through any web browser. Just add pages, paste in your text, upload your images, and then publish. You're even given a full editing interface that anybody familiar with Word will be able to use without any problem—you don't have to worry about any HTML, although you are given the option to edit the code should you need to.

The design and layout of your pages are handled using "Themes." There are thousands of themes available for you to choose from, and you can customize them according to your needs. If you are adept with HTML and CSS, you can create your own themes and apply them to your site.

The core functions of WordPress are often all that you need to create a website, but the functionality can be extended by using plug-ins. There are thousands of plug-ins created by the WordPress community to handle pretty much anything you might need to do.

Content management systems are not suitable for every site. If there are tried-and-tested themes and plug-ins that give the kind of layout and functionality you need, something like WordPress could save you much time and heartbreak. If not, tweaking the system to do your bidding is possible but takes some effort and skill.

Don't reinvent the wheel

There are plenty of sites out there providing free, ready-made resources available to download, which will save time and allow you to focus on the finer details. Check out www.freecsstemplates.org for templates, www.hotscripts.com for features, or www.oscommerce. com for more complex ecommerce functions.

Being able to create a completely bespoke website from scratch is admirable, but you might be able to save yourself a huge amount of time and pain by using ready-made elements that you can easily integrate into your site.

Even professional website designers will base their work on templates and scripts that are tried and tested and can be adapted to the needs of different clients. The use of content management systems is the best example of this: they provide a solid base onto which you can build your site, allowing you to focus more on the design and content.

Even if you don't use the likes of WordPress and Drupal and their associated themes and plug-ins, you will usually be able to find someone that has already done what you are looking to do with your website and is willing to share their work with the world.

A quick search on Google for "CSS templates" will give you a huge number of sites offering free layouts. Two or three columns, fixed-width or fluid, horizontal or vertical navigation . . . pretty much every kind of template you might need will be available for you to download.

You'll also be able to find scripts that will cover all the dynamic features you might want to add, such as contact forms, surveys, charting, and password protection. If just copying and pasting the code into your site seems too much like cheating, there are plenty of tutorials talking you through each step and adapting the functionality to your needs. Hotscripts.com is a good place to start looking for code snippets for almost any scripting language.

Even if you are a coding wizard, there are some areas where it might be advisable to use a third-party solution. Ecommerce is a particularly tricky area, so using an established and reliable solution is often

much wiser than attempting something yourself. A popular free software package is osCommerce (www.oscommerce.com), or you can add simple payment functions into your site using tools provided by Google Checkout (checkout.google.com) or PayPal (www.paypal.com).

Obviously, considerable care has to be taken when downloading and using any software and scripts from the web. They won't always work as they say they will, but worse still you could be inadvertently adding something

malicious to your hard drive. Choose your sources carefully, and look to see how popular or highly rated the downloads are. Check the requirements and do a search to see what problems people have encountered and how they have solved them.

Finding a home

Daily.co.uk is a well-established and affordable hosting provider, but shop around to see who offers the best services and support for your budget.

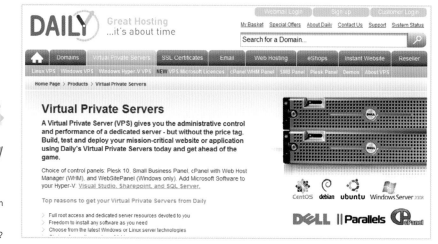

First decision —your host: Unix/Linux or Microsoft?

Before you embark on building your website, you'll have to find somewhere to host it. It's an important decision because it will influence the technologies you use to build the site, and some hosts might impose restrictions that won't let you do what you need.

The first choice to make is Microsoft or Unix/Linux—the platforms used by the hosting provider. Some people will argue vehemently about why one is better than the other, but it will depend on what you are familiar with and what your specific requirements are.

A Microsoft platform—for example, Windows Server 2008—will usually be required if you want to develop .NET applications or use other Microsoft technologies like SQL, but you can often use PHP, MySQL, and other technologies too. Larger businesses will tend to go for Microsoft, as it might fit in with their wider I.T. requirements, and as a result it is often a bit more expensive.

Unix platforms like Linux are usually used for websites using PHP and MySQL. Linux can be much harder to get your head around than Windows, but most Linux hosting packages now come with control panels like Plesk to make things easier.

The next decision will be about the type of hosting:

• Shared hosting: Your site will sit on the same server as many other sites. It will be the cheapest option and simple to manage, but you will have less control and the space and traffic restrictions might be tighter. It will be more than adequate for most small websites, but you will need to set your sights higher if you are looking at something more complex.

• Virtual server: You will have control over the whole server, although there will be many virtual servers on the same machine. You will be able to run multiple sites and applications, but configuring it all is not as straightforward, so you will need some I.T. expertise.

• Dedicated hosting: If you need complete control over the hardware and are running business-critical applications, then you will need your own dedicated machine. A managed hosting package will give you extensive I.T. support and consultancy, but it will be pricey.

Whatever package you go for, look at the web space, database, and traffic restrictions and make sure it will be able to handle your site as it grows.

Selecting which provider to use can be difficult—the larger providers will usually be much cheaper, but you might find plenty of disgruntled customers if you do a quick search on Google. If reliability is crucial to your business, it is worth paying for a hosting solution that gives you 24/7 telephone support and a Service Level Agreement that guarantees up-time.

The right tools for the job

Aptana Studio (www.aptana.com)—a free alternative to Dreamweaver.

The GIMP toolbox—a free alternative to Photoshop.

Professional web design software can be pretty pricey, but thankfully there is almost always a capable, free open-source alternative out there. Sourceforge is one of the best places to start looking: sourceforge.net.

If you are building a website yourself, you need to make sure you are properly equipped. There are hundreds of tools out there to help you with almost anything you want to do with your website, but the key things you will need are a code editor, a graphics package, and software to transfer your files to your web space.

There are plenty of web editing packages available to take the strain out of writing HTML and CSS. Adobe's Dreamweaver is the most widely used editing software out there, but it is also the most expensive. For something a bit more sophisticated—and free—you could try Aptana Studio (www.aptana.com), which lets you develop and test web applications in the same environment.

Many professional web developers will shun the likes of Dreamweaver in favor of simple bare-bones editors like Notepad++ (notepad-plus-plus.org). This might seem like masochism, but editing packages don't always do things as efficiently as you'd want them to.

A text editor means you have full control over the code that is being written, which can give you a better understanding of the workings of your website.

You will need a decent graphics package that will allow you to export web-optimized GIF, JPG, and PNG images. Adobe Photoshop CS is the professional web designer's choice and is an extremely capable bit of software, but it comes at a very high price. Adobe also offers Fireworks, which is more web-focused and a little cheaper, and Xara and Corel also offer quality graphics tools.

If you haven't got money to burn, GIMPshop (www.gimpshop.com) is a modification of the open-source GNU Image Manipulation Programme. While it isn't quite as polished and intuitive as Adobe Photoshop CS, it's completely free.

To transfer files to and from your web server you will need an FTP package. This is often built into software like Dreamweaver, and you can do it through your browser using add-ons like FireFTP for Firefox, but is worth using a dedicated FTP application like FileZilla (filezilla-project.org), which is well-wsupported and free.

Firebug is perhaps the most useful tool in the web-developer's armory, with a wide variety of features to help you test and tweak your web pages. It's a Firefox add-on, but there are "lite" versions for other browsers: www.getfirebug.com.

Chapter 3
Content

018

Content is king

D'Addario offers free music tutorials while Bakerella (www.bakerella.com) gives readers recipes and instructions for making cake accessories.

The most important element of your website is its content, but it is often the thing that gets neglected the most. Your site could be a technical marvel with cutting-edge design, but if it has no content of any real interest or use then people will soon move on.

You should get a grip on your content before you start building your site. How can you start thinking about the navigation if you don't know what it is going to direct people to? How can you start laying out the pages if you don't know what kind of content is going to be on them?

If you have done your research properly, you should have a good idea of what your audience wants to see. You also need to consider what you will actually be able to give them—there's no point creating a page if you won't be able to get anyone to provide the content.

There are some obvious sections that will be included on most websites, but essentially you need to say who you are, what you do, and how you can help your visitors. You want to make it clear how people do what you really want them to when they come to your site, like buy a product, subscribe to a service, get in touch, or come to your real-world location.

Think about what types of content you will be adding to your pages—text, photos, videos, and so on—and how frequently it might be updated. There's little point in having a separate page for events if there will only be one event a year or a photo gallery with just a couple of pictures.

Make sure someone is able to dedicate some time to your site after it has launched. People hate out of date content, and updating your content regularly will mean people are more likely to return to find out what's new.

Don't just focus on what you are selling, consider what else visitors to your site would find useful. For example, if you have a store selling musical instruments, why not provide tutorial videos or care guides like www.daddariobowed.com? Don't be afraid to give away something for nothing—if you can prove your expertise, people are more likely to pay for your services later.

Engaging, useful, and regularly updated content is essential to draw people into your site and keep them coming back for more. Good content is also the cornerstone of search engine optimization—you'll only get listed if your site contains the kinds of things people are searching for, and the better the content, the more likely people will link to your pages.

Writing for the web

Writing for the web is different to writing for print. Most of us have a very short attention span when it comes to reading on screen and we usually scan the page rather than read it word for word. We might look at the first paragraph, but only glance at the rest of the page for headings and words that might be interesting.

As a rule of thumb, you should use about half as many words on a web page as you would in print. Your main heading and first paragraph are the most important text, and they need to concisely describe what the page is about and why it might be interesting to the reader.

You also need to break the page up with short paragraphs and subheadings. Each paragraph should contain just one statement. Don't try to be clever with headings—keep them clear and to the point. Use bulleted lists to show a number of points concisely and highlight keywords and phrases, adding hyperlinks where appropriate.

Avoid too much marketing speak, because people will switch-off very quickly. Focus on the facts and use objective language where possible. Even taglines should be obvious. "Quality wooden toys at an affordable price" is better than something a little more abstract like "Your child's happiness doesn't have to cost the earth," for example.

When writing headlines, make sure the first couple of words include what the subject of the article is about. Eye-tracking studies have shown that people will scan down the left-hand side of text for keywords and might therefore miss them if they are left until the end of the heading.

If you operate in more than one region, you might be looking to provide content in another language. Translation services can be expensive, but the GTranslate plug-in for WordPress and other content management systems uses the impressive Google Translate service to automatically take your text and present it in the language the user selects: edo.webmaster.am/gtranslate.

Remember that people will give up pretty quickly when looking at a webpage, maybe not even making the effort to scroll down, so keep your key text at the top of the page where it's more likely to be noticed.

Your text should focus on what you think your target audience would most want to know, but bear in mind that there could be a vast range of people coming to your site. Where possible, keep the language simple and avoid too many technical terms, especially on the homepage.

There are, of course, occasions when you can break the rules. People might be coming to your website to hear your opinion or be entertained by your wit, and so you should write accordingly. This is particularly the case with blogs and reviews, but even then you need to grab people with a clear headline and punchy opening.

Interactive content

Google Chart Tools
(code.google.com/apis/chart).

Sploder (www.sploder.com).

One of the great things about the web is that you can make it an interactive experience for your visitors. Pages don't just have to be static text and pretty pictures; you can give people choices to make, buttons to press, and games to play.

The rise of user-interface libraries like jQuery means that it easier than ever to add slick interactive elements to your site. You can add complex functions like drag-and-drop, table sorting, selectable tabs, and much more to your pages without needing hardcore development skills. A large community of developers also offer plug-ins for use on

your own site. Don't go crazy though—be sure that anything you add is there to help to make things easier for the user, not more confusing.

There is lots of potential for displaying data in an interactive way, letting your visitors choose what they see and how they see it. So rather than just provide a huge flat table of data and static charts, let people filter the results and set the parameters, and then deliver them with animated effects.

Getting this kind of functionality on your site used to require some hardcore programming and expensive software, but those amazing

programmers at Google have come to the rescue with Google Chart Tools (code.google.com/apis/chart). It's still not really for beginners, but you can get some impressive effects with relatively little effort.

It's easy to think that providing games on your website will give it that added pizzazz —especially if you are targeting a younger audience—but there are so many specialist sites offering top-quality games that you really have to be confident that your offering cuts the mustard before you put it on your site. Sites like Sploder (www.sploder.com) or Yoyo Games (www.yoyogames.com) can help you

Comedy channel Dave offers relevant quizzes for visitors at uktv.co.uk/dave/homepage/sid/7518.

create your own games, or you can license and customize games from providers like WitchHut (www.witchhut.com).

Another option is to provide some kind of quiz with questions that are directly relevant to your site's content. Again, scripts and plug-ins are freely available to help you do that.

Polls are a simple way to get feedback from your audience, to find out what they think about particular issues or the kinds of content they'd like to see. Simple scripts can be embedded into your webpage, or you can download plug-ins for your content management system. Try to make sure your polls are topical and relevant to your content and update them regularly. Also try to show that you have acknowledged the poll results by mentioning them in an article or delivering the kinds of things they have voted for.

Be aware that the results of online polls are not always reliable, so avoid questions that might encourage abuse. Questions like, "Which is the best band?" or similar will always get fans spamming the poll to get their favorite to the top position or a rival to the bottom. Some poll systems can provide some protection against this, but look out for strange voting patterns and be ready to take a poll down if the results begin to look like nonsense.

There is no doubt that interactive content can really give your site an extra edge, but you have to be careful that you don't go too far.

It is tempting to add as many bells and whistles as you can your website, but you still need to focus your content on telling your visitors what they need to know and encouraging them to do what you want them to do. You don't want your interactive features to confuse your visitors or distract them from your key message.

Sound and music

Beat Keep
(www.beatkeep.net).

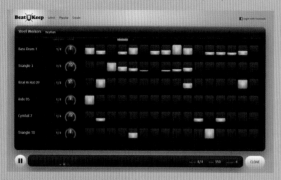

Podsnack
(www.podsnack.com)
provides custom web
audio players that you
can embed into your site.

To really make podcasting
easy you can use services like
Hipcast. This lets you upload
or record online and even phone
in your podcasts. They are then

ready for iTunes, or you can
integrate them with your blog.
Find out more about Hipcast
at www.hipcast.com.

The web is very much a visual medium, and most websites will have no sound at all, but there are times when you might need to provide audio content.

You do have to take particular care when adding sound to your pages. Given that most sites are silent, an unexpected noise like background music or sound effects when you hover over something can be alarming and off-putting. You should restrict your sounds to those that your visitors request—like a recording of an interview or an extract of a song, perhaps.

Embedding sound in your webpage is not always simple either. There are various methods, but some will not work across all browsers. A common method is to use the <embed> tag, but although this is supported by most browsers it is not standards compliant.

Another issue is the fact that different browsers support different file formats, or you have to rely on your visitors having a particular plug-in installed. A popular option is to convert your audio files to Flash and embed a Flash player in your page, as the vast majority of people will have the necessary plug-in to be able to listen your files.

The ideal way to embed audio files in your pages is to use the HTML5 <audio> tag. This is very flexible and allows you do some spectacular things with sound without the need for plug-ins (see www.beatkeep.net). The catch is that HTML5 is only supported by the latest browsers and even then there are some variations in implementation. The <audio> tag is sure to become the standard way to deal with audio content, but until then you should make sure as many people as possible can hear your sound files, so always provide a fallback.

Some audio content is referred to as podcasts, which are simply audio files that are made available for download on your website or through sites like iTunes. Think of them like radio programs you can choose to listen to on your computer or MP3 player whenever you want to.

You don't need fancy technology to make your recordings; a standard USB headset with a microphone will be fine. If you need to edit your files you can use free software like Audacity (audacity.sourceforge.net).

Once recorded, you can provide a link on your webpage to download the podcast as an MP3 file, or you can try reaching further with podcast distribution services. See www.apple.com/itunes/podcasts/specs.html for more details on how to create and distribute your podcast on iTunes.

Providing video content

Developer tools are available to help you better integrate YouTube videos into your website: code.google.com/apis/youtube.

Vimeo is a popular alternative to YouTube for hosting and sharing your video content. It works in much the same way, but video quality tends to be better, and a subscription to the Plus service gives you fewer restrictions and more control over your video content (www.vimeo.com).

What are the YouTube APIs and Tools?

YouTube on any screen, any time. The YouTube APIs and Tools enable you to integrate YouTube's video content and functionality into your website, software application, or device.

Data API

The Data API lets you incorporate YouTube functionality into your own application or website. You can perform searches, upload videos, create playlists, and more.

Player APIs

The Player APIs give you control over YouTube video playback on your website. Configure basic settings, drive the player interface, or even build your own player controls.

Developer Dashboard

The Developer Dashboard shows you at a glance the number of API requests, playbacks, uploads and errors that your app is generating. All you need to do is to provide a developer key in your API requests.

Custom Player

The Custom Player takes you a step beyond just pasting a video into your site. Anyone can easily configure the custom player to show playlists, favorites, or their own videos.

YouTube Direct

YouTube Direct allows you to easily solicit user generated content from your site visitors, moderate the submissions, and display them on your site.

Offering video content was once fraught with difficulties. Not only did you have to worry about cross-browser compatibility and rely on your visitors having the right plug-in installed, but the viewing experience could be ruined by slow dial-up connections.

Now that most of us are on broadband and can even get decent connection speeds while on the move, video content has become much more viable. Providing video content on your site has also become incredibly easy thanks to services like YouTube. You no longer need to worry about formats because YouTube will convert your files for you. They will host your video and provide a player for you to embed in your website. All you need to do is simply cut and paste some code into your page and there it is. YouTube will detect what browser and platform your visitor is using and deliver the video in a format they can view.

It also gives you another way to distribute your content and promote your site. See Chapter 11 on creating a YouTube channel for more.

YouTube does have its limitations, like a maximum video length of fifteen minutes. If you'd rather not let an external service host and deliver your videos, you can embed a video player into your pages.

Flash tends to be the format of choice for video content thanks to its massive install base, but it is not supported by Apple's iOS, so you should think about providing your video using HTML5. The <video> element HTML provides much more than a way to play back your movies on your webpages and will soon be the way most video content is delivered.

One problem with HTML5 video is that there has been no agreement on which formats should be supported. Initially, the specification recommended the Ogg Theora (.ogv) format for video and Vorbis for audio (.ogg), but it has been amended to allow for other formats and MPEG-4/H.264 (.mp4) is now widely used. Unfortunately, different browsers favor different formats and only the latest browsers support HTML5 at all.

To make sure as many people as possible can see your video, you will need to detect what browser is being used and deliver content accordingly. If you go down the HTML5 route, you should provide a Flash fallback. To convert your files to the various formats, you will need software like AVS Video Converter (www.avs4you.com).

Adding a gallery

This is an example of how lightbox and slider plug-ins can be used to great effect to showcase your images in a gallery.

Adding a photo gallery to your site can often be an essential element of your content. If you are selling your artistic skills, you'll need a portfolio to show off your creative talents. You'll also need a collection of photos if you are trying to attract people to your real-world location—be it a hotel, theme park, or desert island—to show how wonderful it is. It is also nice to see that an organization has real people involved, so pictures of successful events with happy people can make your site more welcoming.

A gallery is not always appropriate, however. For example, don't create one if you haven't got enough images to put into it—a half-empty gallery is a waste of a page and won't impress your visitors. If you have a few nice pictures you want to use, it is better to put them in your general content or integrate them in the layout of the page.

All photographic images should be saved as a JPEG and optimized for the web. Without optimization, large file sizes mean you could wait an age for your photos to appear. But don't go too far with the optimization or you'll compromise quality.

Thumbnail images should be created to act as an index for the gallery and should be big enough to give an idea of what the image might be. The main image, whether inside your page content or in a pop-up box, should be a decent-enough size to make an impact but not so big that it might not fit on people's screens.

It goes without saying that you should only use your own photos or images that you have acquired the appropriate rights for—don't just grab pictures you find on Google image search. If you want to protect your own photos, make it clear that they should not be reproduced without permission.

Flickr is a convient option for presenting your gallery. It handles resizing and optimization for you and you can upload via a browser.

That little bit extra: 360-degree panoramas are a great way to display landscapes and building interiors to maximize effect.

You can watermark your images using Adobe Photoshop or cheap software like www.visualwatermark.com, but don't let that spoil a good photo.

Many content management systems come with some kind of photo gallery component, or you can install a variety of plug-ins like NextGEN for WordPress. There are also dedicated image gallery management systems, like Coppermine (coppermine-gallery.net) and Gallery (gallery.menalto.com), that can be integrated with your site.

If you haven't got a content management system, you can create simple galleries with HTML and use something like jQuery to give them some dynamic effects. See www.andrewgransdenphotography.co.uk for good use of lightbox and slider plug-ins.

You could go down the Flash route, creating your own gallery with Action Script or using something like www.flashimagegallery.com, but take care that there is a fallback for visitors who can't view Flash.

One of easiest ways to add photos to your web page is to embed a gallery created with services like Flickr (flickr.com) or Picasa (picasa.google.com). These services let you upload files through a web browser, using your phone or even by email, and then you can share your images with whoever you like, wherever they may be. You'll also get a code snippet that you can add to a web page to display a very effective slideshow. You don't even have to worry about resizing and optimization, as that is all taken care of.

If you really want to try something fancy, you can go for 360-degree panoramas. These are particularly effective for showing the interiors of buildings, like the virtual tours on the English Heritage website (www.english-heritage.org. uk). Services like 360Cities.net offers tips on how you can create panoramas and embed them into your web pages.

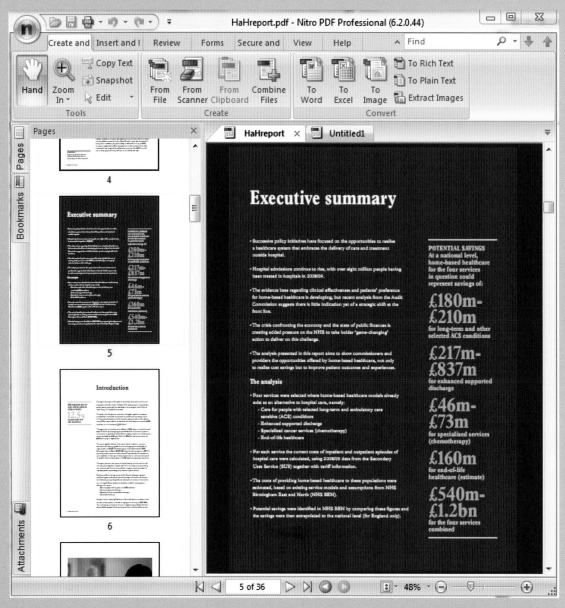

While Adobe Acrobat is the leading software for creating PDFs, cheaper alternatives are available, such as NitroPDF and PrimoPDF. You can download free trial versions to test drive.

Using PDFs
and other documents

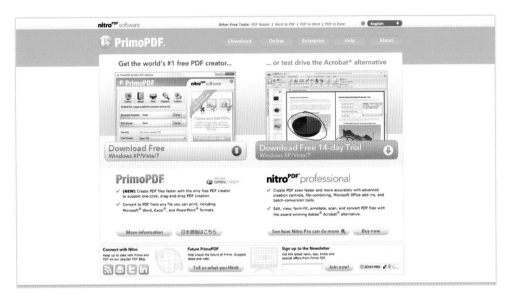

Wherever possible you should present your content in HTML, as it will be quicker and easier to navigate. There are times, however, when you'll want to add links to documents to download, particularly when you are providing electronic versions of printed materials. These could be official reports, magazine articles, posters, and flyers—all content that needs to retain the design and layout of the original and is likely to be printed out and redistributed.

You can link to any type of file, but you have to rely on people being able to open and view it on their computer. You are usually on safe ground with Microsoft Office files, like Word documents or Excel spreadsheets, but the most common document format for downloadable files is PDF. Whatever format is used, it is good practice to show the appropriate icon to indicate what kind of document it is, and for large documents it is good to show the file size too.

In most cases, it is wise to convert your documents to PDF. Nearly everyone will have a PDF viewer installed—even on their mobile phones—and you can prepare files specifically for the web. To be on the safe side, you can provide a discreet link for them to download a viewer if necessary.

Although you can scan documents as PDFs, it is much better to create them from the original documents. To do this you'll need special software. The market-leading package is Adobe Acrobat (www.acrobat.com), but there are much cheaper alternatives like NitroPDF (www.nitropdf.com) or PrimoPDF (www.primopdf.com). The software will let you convert almost any document to PDF, which you will then be able to edit and optimize as necessary.

Search engines are able to index PDF documents, so make sure you add a Google-friendly title, description, and keywords to the document properties. You can also add hyperlinks and create indexes to make navigation easier, although for particularly long documents it might be worth breaking them up into more digestible chunks.

Create a blog

The word "blog" has come into pretty common usage now and comes, of course, from "web log." Blogging is simply the regular publication of news, views, and advice in a reverse chronological order. Blogs are often, but not always, written from a personal perspective and usually invite comments from readers.

There is no doubt that blogs have become a very popular way of publishing content on the web, but do you really need one? Are you going to be able to give it the attention it needs?

It is only worth starting a blog if you think you can spend the time and effort updating it regularly. A blog with a handful of posts, written months ago, is a sorry sight and won't do much for your credibility. Maintaining a blog can be hard work, but keep going and the rewards can be great.

Although blogs can be used to deliver straight news stories or product updates, they are a good way to give a personal touch to your website and interact with your visitors. If you write from your own experiences, offer your opinions, and invite feedback, more people will be more interested to see what you have to say.

Blogs should allow for people to comment on your posts, so be prepared for both positive and negative feedback. You might be able to restrict comments to registered users, or even remove the facility altogether, but interacting with your visitors is one of the most important aspects of blogging. If you give people a voice, they are more likely to come back for more.

Consider who your target audience is and write accordingly. Read over your posts before you submit them, not only to check that they make sense, but also to consider how your comments will be taken. Stimulating a debate is one thing, but rile people too much and you might be bombarded with abuse or alienate the people you want to attract. Off-the-cuff remarks have also landed more than the odd blogger in legal hot water, so think before you post anything too controversial.

Pretty much all blogs are now maintained using a browser-based interface, which means you can easily post articles wherever you may be. Blogging functionality is an integral part of almost all content management systems like WordPress and Drupal, making it simple to get started.

The alternative is to use a hosted blogging service like Blogger.com or WordPress.com (not the self-hosted content management system that is found at WordPress.org). Although much more limited, these services are free and it is easy to set up your first blog. You can choose a theme to complement the design of your site, and then link to your blog from your pages. They also have lots of great advice on creating a successful blog.

If you manage to attend to your blog regularly, it won't be long before you have a wealth of content on your site. Make sure you categorize your posts according to the topic they cover and highlight the most relevant or popular ones to encourage people to delve into your archive.

Bloggers are usually very community spirited, so look around for other blogs in your niche. Make comments on posts, and link to the ones you like. Hopefully they will do the same for you, and soon you could be reaching a much wider audience. Social media sharing is also a key element of blogging, so let anyone who comes across your posts share them with the world through Facebook, Twitter, and the like.

Blogging systems should also offer the facility for people to subscribe to your blog as an RSS feed, meaning they will be able to easily find out whenever you add a post. See Chapter 11, Section 098 on using RSS feeds to promote your site.

All of these connections will do wonders for your search engine optimization, and popular blog posts tend to rank very well on Google.

Create a blog. It's free. [Get started]

    ⟩

Beautiful, customizable templates and layouts. Try the template designer

Up to the minute stats

Make money with Adsense

Explore Blogs of Note

Hosted blogging platforms like Blogger are free and easy to use.

For some real inspiration, check out the winners of the annual Weblog Awards, or "The Bloggies," at 2011.bloggi.es.

Building a discussion forum

The Motley Fool discussion
board at boards.fool.co.uk.

Forum plug-in bbPress
for WordPress at bbpress.org.

The nature of online communities has changed over the years, and although there are still some very popular discussion forums attracting many thousands of visitors, there has been a considerable shift away to the use of blogs and social media.

So why have forums fallen out of favor? Well, it is extremely difficult to get a forum off the ground. It's a chicken and egg situation—people will only read and post on a forum if lots of other people have already contributed. This means that you have to create a variety of relevant topics and post useful comments to them yourself. You then have to encourage anyone you know to post comments, and then hope they spread the word. It is hard work, but the goal is to reach that critical mass of users that will mean it takes care of itself.

The most successful forums are usually advice sites. The discussion boards at The Motley Fool are very active with people

seeking and giving financial advice, and the massive community they built means they can expand into broader lifestyle topics: boards.fool.co.uk.

Forums are also useful for customer support. You could provide topics for the most frequently asked questions and then ask customers to submit queries to the forum. Any answers you give will then be available to everyone else, and others might even be able to offer advice for you.

The biggest issue with forums is being able to control what people write. You don't want disgruntled customers broadcasting their issues to the world, and you don't want people to spam your boards with irrelevant or unsuitable content.

Moderation is essential, so you can go in and edit or remove unwanted comments, but it can be a full-time job if you are lucky enough to have an active forum. You can reduce this

to a degree if you insist that people register before posting, but that just provides a barrier to new people making a contribution.

You can go further by not publishing any comments before they have been authorized first, but unless you can publish comments soon after they are made, people will get fed up with your site and not bother to return.

Whether you moderate the comments or not, you have to take care that people are not saying anything libelous or offensive on your site, because it is you who could take the responsibility.

There are a variety of forum packages available, the most popular being the free and open-source phpBB (www.phpbb.com). Plug-ins are also available for content management systems, such as bbPress for WordPress (bbpress.org).

Offering subscriber-only content

Although we have all become very used to getting much of our web diet for nothing, some content is worth paying for.

It is still difficult to make money by charging for content, but the tide does seem to be turning. Major publishers are now requiring payment for publications like *The New York Times*, and although overall traffic may have fallen, the online editions now appear to be paying their way.

Even if your subscription content is inexpensive or free, any kind of registration process presents a barrier to your users. People usually expect to find what they are looking for without being presented with a form asking for their details. Some will be put off and look elsewhere.

You have to be sure that your content really is desirable enough for them to make the effort to get at it. Think about whether they can get the same stuff elsewhere but without the hassle or expense.

If you still believe that your content is worth a subscription, give them a taster of what they can expect if they sign up. If you can provide some useful information for nothing and make your premium content sound great, then people are more likely to give it a go.

Putting content behind a login isn't all about making money, of course. You might have content that provides added value to your customers or is simply something that you don't want to make available to the general public.

Whether or not your company has an intranet, you could use your website as an "extranet" to provide information for employees. For example, regional sales people who are not based in the office could login to access marketing material or product demos to show to clients.

Many news sites now charge for certain content through a subscription fee.

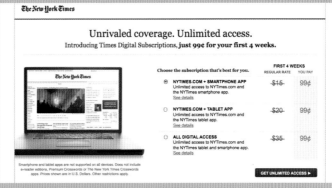

Professional bodies like the Institute of Chartered Accountants allow members to log in to update their profile or access training records: www.icaew.com.

They wouldn't have to worry about having the relevant files with them all the time because they could simply view or download the very latest version wherever they can get online.

If you plan on putting sensitive or confidential material online, take care that you have sufficient security in place and make sure your users choose strong passwords that they review regularly.

One problem with subscription-only content is that the search engines are not subscribers.

Some of your most relevant and valuable pages could be hidden, so consider carefully what needs to be behind the wall.

To help get around this issue, Google offers a service that allows you to index subscriber-only content. First Click Free lets Google users see the first subscriber-only article it comes across in search results but will then prompt people to sign up if they try to go elsewhere on the site. See www.google.com/support/webmasters/bin/answer.py?answer=74536 for more information.

The other alternative is to provide snippets of the full articles on pages that don't require a login, so that this content can be indexed by the search engines. Subscribers could then follow a link to read more.

Chapter 4
Navigation

The principles of navigation

Navigation is perhaps the most important element of your website, because people won't hang around long if they can't find their way around. You need to tell your visitors where to go, where they are, and where they have been, and make it all as clear and easy to use as possible.

You don't want your visitors to think too hard when they come to your site, so the navigation has to be intuitive. There are many different ways you can do it, but your visitors will need to immediately recognize how it all works. It usually pays to follow convention—if you try something they have not seen before, then that could cause some confusion.

Consistency is particularly important as it helps the user to become familiar with the site and understand its structure quickly, so it is good practice to keep your primary navigation appearance and basic functionality the same for every page of your site. You won't necessarily need a secondary navigation for all pages, but where it is used it should appear in the same place each time, such as in a right sidebar.

Your key navigation items should be clearly visible and properly labeled at all times—you don't want the link to only be revealed when you hover over a particular element. The more you make the user guess, the less likely it is you'll keep them on the site. There may be constraints within your design that simply don't allow for all the top-level elements to be displayed, but if this is the case then perhaps you need to look at simplifying the structure.

From a markup perspective, your navigation should be an unordered (<ul>) list, with each list item containing a link to the relevant page. Use CSS to determine its position and style, but it should still be properly nested and make sense if the CSS is disabled. To improve the semantics further, HTML5 has introduced the <nav> tag to indicate a group of links that point to other parts of the site, and this should be wrapped around your list.

Avoid using images for navigation items, especially for text. You can still use background images, but using normal text styled accordingly is much better in terms of accessibility and efficiency. Keep the design simple and the labels easy to scan and read, with sufficient contrast between the text and the background.

And beware of relying on JavaScript, or code that is not supported across all browsers and devices, to make your navigation work, because some people could soon become stuck and leave very quickly.

Getting the structure right

While you were planning your website, you will have created a sitemap on paper that details all the sections you want and how they are connected. It is important to get this right before you build anything, because it will drive how the site is designed and changing it further down the line might not be so easy.

Most websites have a structure built on three levels: the homepage, the main sections, and the subsections. The homepage will convey the purpose of the site and highlight key content, and the main sections should be broad but obvious and act as gateways into the more specific content held in the subsections.

Abercrombie & Fitch have clearly labeled sections and subsections in their sitemap, helping visitors easily find what they are looking for: www.abercrombie.com.

For example, an online fashion store might have broad areas like "Men," "Women," and "Children" for the main sections, with "Coats," "Shoes," "Jeans," and so on as subsections. But if the store only dealt with children's clothes, those subsections might be at the higher level instead.

You also need to think about where news articles or products will fit into your structure, but you don't need to list all of these at this stage because they should be ever-changing once you have launched your site.

Larger sites might need further levels in the hierarchy, but bear in mind that this will start to make your navigation more complex and could make it harder for people to find what they are looking for.

If you only envisage half a dozen pages of content or less, you won't need subsections at all, making the navigation very simple.

But you need to consider how your site might grow and so think about how you could extend the navigation should you need to in the future.

You should try to balance your hierarchy as best you can—it can look odd if one or two sections have a dozen subsections and the rest have none. Try to limit the number of items at each level, as it makes them much harder to scan. Six main sections with six subsections each is much easier to deal with than, say, twelve main sections with the same number of items below that. Additionally, avoid single subsections; you should be able to fit all content at the higher level rather than create more pages.

Canon's website features two
tiers of horizontal navigation
at the top: www.canon.com.

Vertical navigation can work well
if you have a fairly minimalist
design and limited content, where
space isn't so much of an issue:
www.publishedbyprocess.com.

Not so long ago, the majority of websites probably had the primary navigation—the menu that will appear on every page of your site—in a column on the left-hand side. More recently, web design convention has shifted toward a horizontal navigation across the top of the page, and some web designers will insist that a vertical navigation should be avoided at all costs.

The biggest argument against vertical navigation is that it wastes valuable screen space. That is certainly a valid point, and there are many websites that have half a dozen items and then a big empty space alongside a long block of text. A bit of white space can enhance a design, for sure, but not when you have to cram content in elsewhere. There are times when you need to make the most of what width you have, particularly if you are displaying tables or large images.

Another argument against left-hand navigation is that, because we naturally scan down the left-hand side of the page, a vertical navigation takes the focus away from what you really want people to see. You certainly want the navigation to be noticeable, but it is more important to draw attention to the content. A horizontal

navigation is compact and easily visible where people expect to find it at the top of the page. You then have the freedom to make the most of the space below to show off your content.

If you have a dynamic menu that displays a list of sub-items when you hover over the link, it is probably better to have those as dropping down from the top rather than flying out from the side. Most of us will also recognize the down-arrow icon as an indicator for a drop-down menu, but a right arrow could mean a number of things, such as a fly-out, or it could also indicate a link to an external site.

The default option for most content management systems will be a horizontal navigation, and you'll find that most of the themes available will go the same way. On balance, it is probably the best choice for most sites, but that doesn't mean it makes sense for everyone.

One possible problem with a horizontal navigation is that you might not have room to grow. Ideally you'd want those main navigation items to stay pretty fixed, whatever option you choose, but it is sometimes difficult to predict how things will develop.

You could start with a design where you have six equally sized navigation items that stretch across the full width of your design—but what happens when you need to add a seventh? Can you just reduce the width of each item? Will you need to change the font size or create a new background image? These might not be huge issues to solve, but it is usually much easier to add extra items to a vertical navigation.

Horizontal navigation also doesn't handle long headings very well, because you soon start to run out of space to fit in all the text. You should try to be as succinct as you can, of course, but that isn't always possible. Also consider whether your site will be translated into different languages, as this could affect the length of words used in your navigation. If your items are in a column, you have a little more flexibility and can even wrap on to another line if necessary.

For larger navigations, a vertical position makes it simpler to group different items to make them easier to identify. You are likely to see vertical navigation on ecommerce sites, where there is often a long list of product . categories with labels of varying length, and these could change considerably over time.

Extending the navigation

The British Library's website is a good example of how a "mega drop-down" menu can be used to include a lot of content, without sacrificing the use of simple horizontal navigation: www.bl.uk.

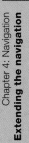

Working out where to put your primary navigation items is one problem, but where do you show the next level down? Are all sub-items visible, or do you have to click on a section to reveal them? Do you create a drop-down menu or list them on the row below?

A common approach is to have the main navigation items across the top, but the links relevant to each section appear in a menu in a separate column on the right or left of the page. This can give you the best of both worlds for horizontal and vertical navigation, allowing you the space to make the most of your homepage but offering the flexibility to expand and use longer headings elsewhere on your site.

You do have to take some care not to lose your visitors while they negotiate from one level to the next—it should be clear where they are and where they need to look next for further content, and that might not be so obvious if you separate the secondary from the primary navigation.

Drop-down menus are a familiar way to navigate around a website, but you don't want the lists to get too long. If you have a lot of content to flag up, a good option is to use a "mega drop-down." This lets you keep a horizontal navigation bar but offers some of the flexibility of vertical navigation by enabling you to list a large number of items and group them as necessary.

You might need to provide links to pages that aren't quite so important to sit in the primary navigation but still apply to the whole site, and so wouldn't be suitable in a subsection. This will include things like the terms and conditions, privacy policy, accessibility statements, and the like, but it could also be links to the "about us" page or other background information—namely content that is not directly relevant to what your visitors want from your site. These additional

navigation links will commonly be placed in the footer, but you will also see them discreetly placed at the top of the page on some sites.

You don't want to have too many levels of navigation, but there are some elements that are only relevant to certain pages and don't fit neatly into your site structure. On blogging sites in particular, you will see links to latest articles, archives, and alternative categories, all dynamic items that will automatically change over time. These kinds of items are generally found in a sidebar, and you might also want this area to highlight related links or documents, particularly those on external sites.

Splitting content by audience

The Healthcare at Home website has several different audiences that it needs to reach but has a site that manages to welcome them all. The homepage clearly asks what information you are looking for and directs you the right way. The main navigation is consistent through the site with a drop-down menu that links to all the different areas: www.hah.co.uk.

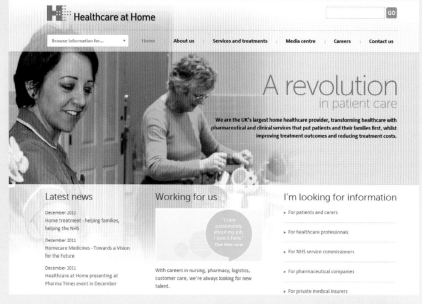

One issue you might have to deal with is providing different content for different audiences. For example, your organization might want to engage with the public but also want to deal with professionals, or you might want to provide different content for different regions or languages.

The way some organizations deal with this is to have a global homepage that asks the visitor which content they'd like to see and then leads them to the appropriate version of the site, each with its own navigation and design. This is not ideal, as you are just creating another step for people before they get to content they want, and you are effectively creating multiple websites to build and maintain. And what if someone doesn't

fit nicely into one audience or the other? Will they have to switch back and forth between the sites to get what they need?

It is much better to create a single website that caters for all types of visitor. You should be able to create a navigation that defines which content is for whom and a homepage that directs people to the different areas of your site. This not only makes life easier for you and your visitors, but having a single site to promote will be better for your search-engine rankings.

Another way you can split content by audiences is through registration. For example, a professional organization might want to provide some content for its members only and will therefore ask them to login

before they can access it. This could mean that some navigation items might not be visible to the general public, but you need to ensure that the navigation still works in the same way and fits into the design for both audiences. Another option is to keep all navigation items visible, but indicate which ones require a login.

Some sites will do this by graying out the items or showing a key to indicate that access is restricted, but a better way is to group them in a single section helpfully labeled "Member services" or something similarly obvious.

You are here

The Guardian website effectively combines breadcrumb trails with its main horizontal navigation and uses color-coding to great effect: www.guardian.co.uk.

San Francisco's Exploratorium site combines a tabbed navigation with a breadcrumb trail and other signs to show you exactly where you are. www.exploratorium.edu.

As people navigate around your site it is helpful to give them an indication of exactly where they are. The most obvious signs are clear headings and page titles that describe the content on that page. These should be consistent with any links your visitors have followed to get to the page or else people might think they have not arrived at the content they were expecting.

The main navigation should also reflect the current page, so that the relevant item is highlighted in a different color or in bold text. You could also use a tabbed effect, which joins the navigation heading to the content below to make it clear what section you are in.

Never remove the current page from the navigation, even though people won't need to follow a link to a page they are already on. If the navigation changes from page to page, it'll just confuse your visitors.

Another useful navigational technique to help people get their bearings is to use breadcrumb trails. Rather than show people where to go, breadcrumbs show them the path to where they are now and gives them the opportunity to easily retrace their steps—just like Hansel and Gretel in the fairy tale. They also highlight exactly where you are in the site's structure, which is particularly helpful if people have landed at a page lower down in the hierarchy.

Breadcrumb trails typically sit above the page heading, running horizontally to take up as little room as possible. They should just use simple text with each element separated with

a ">" or other appropriate symbol and be large enough to read clearly without distracting too much from the main navigation. CSS can be used for the separators using the :before and :after pseudo-classes.

Only use breadcrumb trails if you have lots of content organized into many different categories in a logical hierarchy. There is no point using them if your site's structure has no more than one or two levels, and they will not work well if some content fits into more than one category. If you do use breadcrumbs, they should only ever be a feature that complements your main navigation, not replaces it.

That being said, The Guardian newspaper's website manages to combine a breadcrumb

trail with its main navigation, effectively showing where each section sits in a very complex structure while still signposting the way to content deeper down. It also color codes each section, so red is for news, green is for sports, and so on.

Another way to indicate where people have been is to change the color of visited links. This is something that will happen by default if you don't change the CSS, but you will see many sites that will make all links the same color to simplify the color scheme. This is not a tragedy, but even a subtle change on those visited links can help people see what they have already done and highlight content they have yet to look at.

Dynamic effects

There are plenty of places to find free code snippets and plug-ins to create dynamic menus, but it's worth taking a look at the premium examples at code canyon.net. They are rarely more than a few dollars a time, but it can just be a good place to give you ideas of what you can do on your own.

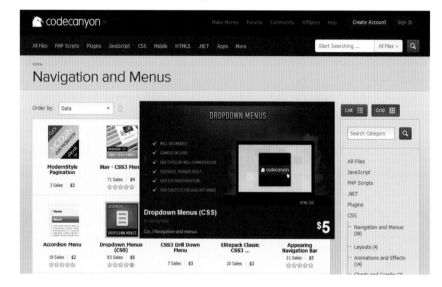

Many sites will now take advantage of JavaScript libraries like jQuery to create an impressive range of dynamic effects for the navigation. This could vary from simple drop-down menus to concertinas that expand and contract as you click on the main items, with nice smooth animation that can give your site a really polished feel.

Some care has to be taken if you use JavaScript on your navigation menus, however, because you don't want your lovely effects to make it harder for people to navigate your site. For a start, you need to make sure that they still work as menus if JavaScript is turned off—it's easy to think that pretty much everybody will have JavaScript enabled in their browser, but you can't always rely on the script being delivered and rendered as you want. People

using screen readers and other assistive devices could end up being stranded, and there are other platforms where your navigation might not work as you intended. You'll also want search engines to be able to follow all links on your navigation so that they can index your site.

JavaScript isn't always the answer when it comes to adding dynamic effects, and there is plenty you can do with CSS and HTML alone. One of the most common effects is to change the appearance of each navigation item when you hover over it to give users some visual feedback to what they are doing. This can easily be done using CSS, swapping to an alternate background color or image, and is a much better approach than using JavaScript to create an image rollover effect. But you can go much further with CSS to

create drop-downs, fly-outs, and tab menus, and all should be more efficient and reliable than using JavaScript.

In summary, script usage should be considered only as a visual enhancement for the user, not as core functionality; so start with the HTML and add presentation layers progressively to the basic design. CSS should be your priority, with JavaScript being the final "cherry on top," if required, rather than it providing any core functionality.

Some mobile devices struggle with dynamic elements and the small screen can make some menus difficult to use. You might opt for some kind of mobile detection—which we will cover later—to provide a more appropriate navigation for these devices.

Using icons

CampaignMonitor
makes good use of icons
to highlight key features:
www.campaignmonitor.com.

Icons are images that suggest the function of the content they are associated with. They are often easier to scan than text alone and so can help people quickly find what they are looking for.

They can be used to make headings stand out and reinforce their meaning, to draw attention to particular content, and to distinguish between different products and services. They can also be used to replace text where space is limited, such as controls for playing a video or for editing functions.

It should be obvious what an icon represents, so stick with convention and use metaphors that people are likely to understand: a house for the homepage, a question mark for help, a speech bubble for comments, and so on. That's not always so easy for some content, and certain images can mean different things to different people. If in doubt, keep things neutral and avoid using icons that could be confused for something else, but don't try to shoehorn an icon in where it just doesn't work.

Icons design should be clear and simple with no unnecessary elements. You shouldn't need to use text on an icon unless it is a recognizable acronym or branding. Take care when using effects like drop shadows or gradients as they can take away some of the clarity on small images. Icons should match the look and feel of the rest of the site, have a consistent size and shape, and look as though they all come from the same set.

Try not to rely too much on icons in isolation; one can be used without any associated text, but if so it is even more important to make its meaning obvious. Icons can be links, but it is helpful if there is some visual clue that the icon is active when you hover over it.

Designing a decent set of icons is harder than it looks, so it's fortunate that there are plenty of designers out there willing to share their efforts with you.

Iconfinder.com, with hundreds of professional-looking sets that cover the most common icons you will need, is one of the best places to start your search.

Effective homepages

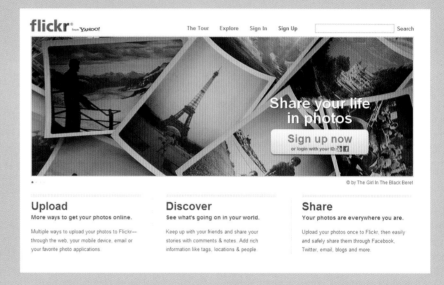

By having a sign-in function, Flickr is able to tailor the homepage to new visitors or returning users.

Your homepage will often be the first thing a new visitor will see when they come to your site, so it is crucial it that makes a positive impact. But the homepage is also an important element of your navigation, as it will highlight the key areas you want people to visit.

You need to consider what it is you want to achieve from your website and use your homepage to focus on those goals. Even if they have arrived at your site on a different page, people will often go back to the homepage to get their bearings and decide where to go next.

Keep everything simple and avoid trying to cram everything you can into one page—you should just be highlighting key content and leading your visitors to other pages on your site.

Use a large, strong image that shows off what you are offering and gives the best possible impression.

When people come to your homepage they want to be sure that your site provides what they are looking for, so you need a meaningful headline and an introduction that succinctly explains the purpose of your site. Just writing "Welcome" isn't particularly helpful, nor is a detailed explanation of who you are. A couple of sentences should be enough to sum up what you are offering, along with a clear indication of what they need to do next to get what they want.

As well as making it obvious what you do, you'll want to encourage people to visit again and again. Your homepage isn't just for new visitors, it's a place for telling those returning

what is new and what they can expect soon, so highlight the latest developments, news stories, and special offers. If everything looks the same as it did the last time they visited, they might not bother to pop by again.

If you have a subscription service, you could offer different homepages to new visitors and those who have signed up. Take Flickr: the homepage is focused on getting you to register, but once you have logged in it is all about what is new and encouraging you to engage with the community.

Whatever you do, don't create a splash page where someone has to click "enter the site" before they get into anything useful. No matter how amazing your animated splash page might be, it serves no useful purpose and will just end up being an annoyance.

Adding a search facility

Before you add a search facility to your website, you have to think whether it is really necessary. If you have clear navigation and only a handful of pages, then your visitors should easily be able to find what they want without needing to turn to a search box. But if you have a wealth of content that is growing every day, then people will need a little extra little help to find what they want. In fact, for the most complex websites, the search might end up being the most used method of navigation.

Most content management systems will offer a decent enough search facility as standard, but you will usually be able to get plug-ins or modules that extend the default functionality.

If you are not using a content management system, and if building your own search facility sounds beyond your talents, then the easiest option is to embed Google's Custom Search on your site.

This gives a variety of templates that you can customize to best fit with your design theme, and you can choose from several layout options. You'll then get the code to paste into the appropriate page on your site. It's extremely simple, but if the limited options don't give you what you need you can download the source code and tweak the JavaScript and CSS to customize it further.

There are a few optional features that can be useful, including auto-completion and promotion boxes that are triggered by a particular query. You can even search multiple sites with one search.

The standard edition of Google Custom Search is free, but adverts will be shown besides the search results. You can disable ads if you are a non-profit organization, but you can also make money from them through Google's AdSense For Search program. The Site Search edition

Most search functions sit in the top right corner of a website, and often feature a magnifying glass icon, as seen on cnet.co.uk.

Customize your search facilty by choosing one from Google Custom Search, then copy and paste the code to your own site.

starts at $100, but costs will increase depending on the number of search queries that are run on your site. This premium version is ad-free and has extra features and greater customization options. For very large sites with high traffic, you'll need to look at Google's enterprise solutions.

However you implement search on your site, you need to make sure that it is easy to find and use. The usual position for the search box is the top right of the page, and it needs to be obvious what it is for.

Don't get clever with the design; keep it simple with an input field that stands out and a clear submit button labeled "Search" or a recognizable icon like a magnifying glass. The input field should be big enough for visitors to add plenty of text, and it should be clear what they are typing.

One technique often used is to add grayed-out text to indicate what kinds of things they can search for, but make sure this sample text disappears when they start to enter their own query. If you are working in HTML5, you might consider using the "placeholder" attribute to

provide this text, as modern browsers will automatically hide the text rather than using a JavaScript-based solution.

Filters can be helpful alongside some search boxes, but often it just overcomplicates things—people generally just want to enter a word and go. Auto-complete functionality can also be useful, particularly when searching for the names of people or places, but again make sure that it doesn't get in the way of a simple search.

The results page should list content in some kind of logical order, usually relevance, but it could be by date or popularity. Further sorting options or filters can be helpful to narrow down the results. The search query used should be shown at the top of the page with an opportunity to refine or change the search criteria. The titles should be clear links to the relevant page, but there should also be a short description for each results entry.

You can limit the number of results shown on each page, but indicate how many results there are in total and clearly show how they can navigate to further pages.

The website for a company as large as Apple, with such a wealth of products and services on offer, benefits from an extensive sitemap.

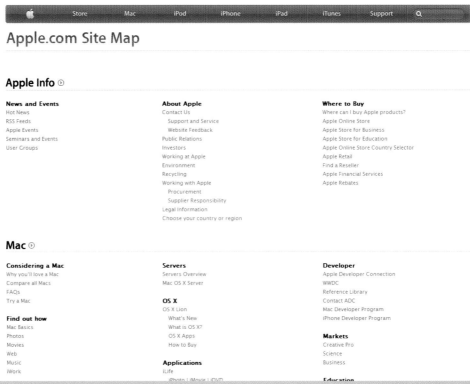

Apple.com Site Map

Apple Info ⊙

News and Events
Hot News
RSS Feeds
Apple Events
Seminars and Events
User Groups

About Apple
Contact Us
  Support and Service
  Website Feedback
Public Relations
Investors
Working at Apple
Environment
Recycling
Working with Apple
  Procurement
  Supplier Responsibility
Legal Information
Choose your country or region

Where to Buy
Where can I buy Apple products?
Apple Online Store
Apple Store for Business
Apple Store for Education
Apple Online Store Country Selector
Apple Retail
Find a Reseller
Apple Financial Services
Apple Rebates

Mac ⊙

Considering a Mac
Why you'll love a Mac
Compare all Macs
FAQs
Try a Mac

Find out how
Mac Basics
Photos
Movies
Web
Music
iWork

Servers
Servers Overview
Mac OS X Server

OS X
OS X Lion
What's New
What is OS X?
OS X Apps
How to Buy

Applications
iLife
iPhoto | iMovie | iDVD

Developer
Apple Developer Connection
WWDC
Reference Library
Contact ADC
Mac Developer Program
iPhone Developer Program

Markets
Creative Pro
Science
Business

Education

The website for celebrity chef Jamie Oliver features a simple footer menu bar, as well as a list of helpful shortcuts. The sitemap page offers a further list of options: www.jamieoliver.com.

jamie oliver group

shortcuts

Jamie
• News
• Diary
• Biography

Recipes
• Recipes
• Member recipes

Shop
• Jme Shop
• Mobile apps
• Jamie Oliver Products
• Wood Fired Ovens

Books & TV
• Jamie's Great Britain
• Jamie's 30 Minute Meals
• Jamie Does
• Jamie's American roadtrip
• Jamie at Home
• Cook with Jamie
• Jamie's Italy

Restaurants
• Barbecoa
• Recipease
• Jamie's Italian
• Fifteen
• Fabulous Feasts

Campaigns
• Jamie's Food Revolution
• Ministry of Food
• School Dinners

Share
• Forums
• Blogs
• RSS

Party plan
• Jamie at Home

More
• Home Cooking Skills
• Magazine
• FreshOne Productions
• Tonic Productions
• Gardening
• Wine
• Videos
• Toolbar

Terms & Conditions | Privacy Policy | Customer Services | Sitemap | Advertise | Help | Careers with Jamie

Sitemaps

If you have prepared properly, you will have created a sitemap on paper while planning your navigation, showing all the sections on your site and how the content is structured. You can turn all that into HTML and add a sitemap page to provide another way of navigating your site.

Your sitemap doesn't have to include every page on your site, but it should list all the main sections. Just like any other content, it should be organized logically and labeled clearly. Short descriptions of each page can be helpful, but titles should be links and obvious enough for people to know what to expect when they follow them.

If your content is updated regularly, then amending the sitemap every time you add a new post can be a chore and might make the page too unwieldy to be useful. But if you add new sections, change the structure of your site, or remove pages, then remember to edit the sitemap accordingly. It can be very confusing for people if your content is not where you say it is, and Google isn't going to look kindly on broken links.

Rather than have a separate sitemap page, a common trend is to add your sitemap to the foot of every page. This might mean it's more likely to be seen and used, but you don't want it to distract from the main navigation and content, so keep the design simple and headings brief.

If your main navigation is already crystal clear and your search facility lets people quickly find what they are looking for, you might think that providing another page of links for your visitors is unnecessary. The most common argument for creating a sitemap is not so much for aiding navigation but for search engine optimization; the idea being it provides a handy place for all those search bots to find all the content on your website. How effective it is in reality is open to debate, but it certainly can't hurt to include one.

Where a sitemap can be particularly useful is when you have lots of dynamic content that the search engine robots can't normally find—for example, if you have a directory where all the content is held in a database and accessed using an internal search facility. You can open all this up to the search engines if you create a sitemap that has links to every entry in the database, like an alphabetical list of people or companies.

As long as the sitemap can be indexed, then all of those entries can be indexed too, which can make a huge difference to your search engine performance.

You'll find more details on how sitemaps can improve your search-engine ranking in Chapter 11.

Chapter 5
Layout

Organizing your page

The box model lets you control your layout by changing the CSS properties of each box.

There are three main tried-and-tested layouts for web pages.

Laying out a web page is like organizing a series of boxes. You have an overall box for the container and within that you'd generally have boxes for the header, the content, and the footer. There will usually be many other boxes inside those, like ones for the navigation, sidebars, search, and so on, but you can think of all elements as rectangular boxes including headings, paragraphs, and list items.

All of these boxes can be controlled by the CSS and can have a width and height for the content, padding inside the box, and a border and a margin around the box. Different settings can apply to each side of the box, or you don't have to have any border, margin, or padding at all. Margins are always transparent, but you can set the style of borders and apply a background color or image for the area within the borders.

The boxes will flow vertically one on top of the other unless you specify otherwise. You can give a box an absolute position, measured from the top left corner of the browser window, or a relative position where you place where it should go relative to where it would normally go. Boxes can also be floated left or right, which means that any elements following it will flow around it. For example, you could float an image so that the text wraps around it.

Understanding the box model and the way elements are positioned is key to mastering web page layout, so if you are a novice designer get to grips with how it all works before you start.

If you've got all that covered, you'll know that CSS offers a huge amount of control over your design and gives you the flexibility to choose any kind of layout you might want. Commonly you'll see a two-column design, with a header across the top, the main content below in one column, and a smaller column on the right, but you could go for a single column, three columns, or a grid of equally sized boxes.

There isn't a right or wrong option, but there is a good reason why you see the same layouts over and over again. Anything out of the ordinary can confuse your viewers and too many page elements can be hard to take in.

Whichever layout you choose, everything should be arranged neatly and well spaced out. Make sure you have sufficient padding and margins on your elements, particularly around text, otherwise everything starts to look cluttered. As we will see later on, you can use grids to help keep things tidy and properly aligned.

Don't be afraid of white space on your page—you might be tempted to squeeze in as much content as you can, but this can make it hard to distinguish elements from each other and to read text. Of course, you can go too far the other way; leaving large gaps in the content can make it look like something is missing.

The biggest issue you will have to deal with when laying out your page is getting it to work properly for everyone who sees it. Your visitors will be using a variety of web browsers and could be viewing it on very different screens, so all that has to be taken into consideration when arranging all those boxes.

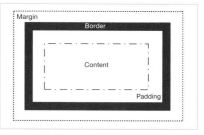

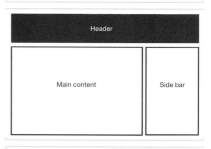

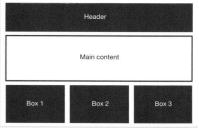

Thinking above the fold

Broadsheet newspapers typically lay out their pages so that the masthead and most important headlines are "above the fold" and they can be seen on the newsstand. You can apply a similar principle to web design, putting the header and key content at the top of the page where it is more likely to catch the eye.

But where exactly is the fold on a web page? It will depend on each viewer's screen resolution of course, but also the browser they are using, the settings they've chosen, and the toolbars they have installed will affect how much of the web page actually shows on the screen. There is little point in trying to get particular elements to fit exactly to your own screen, because other people's views are likely to be different.

Some things should definitely be visible without most people needing to scroll down. This should include your branding, conventionally in the top left corner, but note that most people expect a logo to act as a link back to the homepage, even if you have a link on your navigation. You'd also expect to see a login button and search box, if that is relevant for your site, and it is good to highlight your key contact points. You should also make sure the main navigation is all on show—an advantage of a horizontal navigation bar, as discussed in Chapter 4.

It still makes sense to keep the most important body content nearer the top of the page, but you should not get too hung up on it. It is better to have larger text that is well spaced and easy to read than have everything all squashed up to fit above the imaginary and unpredictable fold.

One reason for keeping your top content high up on the page is to reduce the amount of scrolling required. Although it is perhaps no longer quite so relevant. These days large monitors and scroll-wheel mice are much

more commonplace, and tablet devices positively encourage you touch the screen to see more.

It seems that people really don't mind scrolling that much, and most of us will happily go down to the bottom of the longest pages, even if we are only skimming through the content to see what is there.

The Museum of Modern Art tries a different approach to above-the-fold design by making sure the navigation is always visible at the foot of the page, whatever the screen size, or however much you scroll down. This means that the key content is always right at the top: www.moma.org.

Fixed vs. flexible layouts

Amazon.com employs a flexible layout with three columns and fixed widths for the sidebars. Only the central content expands.

See mediaqueri.es for great examples of adaptive web design.

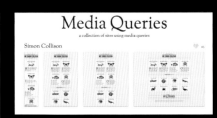

Not everyone will be looking at your web pages in the same way—some will be using massive HD monitors while others will be squinting at tiny netbook screens. You need to lay out your web pages in a way that works for as many people as possible, but you will have to decide how you achieve that, namely, with a fixed layout or a flexible one.

A fixed layout means that the overall width of your web page will be the same for everyone, whatever the size of their screen. You'll want people to view your page without having to scroll horizontally, so you need to set a width that caters for the vast majority of your visitors.

The majority of people now have a screen width of at least 1280 pixels, but the widely accepted web-design norm is to have a fixed-width of around 960–970 pixels which, accounting for scroll bars, will fit nicely at the still-common 1024 pixel resolution. Some people will be stuck at an even lower resolution, but setting shorter widths can make your pages look a little narrow for many users—particularly those with larger screen resolutions—and could limit what you can do with your design.

With flexible—or fluid—layouts, the overall width is set as a percentage and so the view will change for each user depending on their screen size. Not all elements on the page necessarily need a relative width; for example, a flexible layout with three columns could have fixed widths for the sidebars and only the central content section expanding, just like Amazon.

Fixed layouts are probably the most popular choice for web designers, because they tend to be easier to work with. You can be more precise about your design and more confident that your users will see your site as you want them to see it. The problem is that at very high resolutions, you can have large gaps either side of your content making your design look a bit lost. Good use of page backgrounds can help this, but the images need to be wide enough to accommodate the widest of resolutions.

Flexible layouts can work better in terms of usability and accessibility, but can be hard to get right. The main issue is that you don't have so much control over how things will look for different people. The way text wraps around

images will depend on the overall width of the screen and images themselves might look out of proportion. Again, larger screen resolutions can pose a problem, because it can be very difficult reading very long lines of text and you might get too much blank space if you don't have much content on the page. To make sure key elements don't scale in such a manner as to become unreadable, minimum and maximum widths can be set in the CSS.

Another option is to use an adaptive layout, which has many of the benefits of both the fixed and flexible options but with fewer potential problems. Adaptive layouts can be built using CSS3's @media query to detect what screen dimensions your user has and serve an appropriate style sheet. Creating different layouts for a variety of screen dimensions is no doubt more effort, and we must remember that CSS3 is still not fully supported, but it is worth thinking about adaptive layouts especially if you want to cater for mobile users—which we will go into later in this chapter.

Keeping it in proportion

Artists and architects have long recognized that some things look better if the proportions are just so. There is even a mathematical formula they use to calculate the relative sizes of two objects called the golden ratio, and this magical number is approximately 1.618. Why this measure makes designs so aesthetically pleasing is hard to say, but there is no doubt that it has been used for centuries in many of history's greatest works.

So how can the golden ratio be used in the design of your humble web page? Say you plump for a two-column, fixed-width layout, with the main content in one column and your secondary navigation in another. If your fixed width is 960px, then one column should be 960 divided by 1.618, so rounded down this would be 593px. The second column would therefore be 367px. The golden ratio can also be applied to set height relative to the width of an element, so a box that is 300px wide should be 185px high to follow the rules of this "divine proportion."

Another rule many artists will stick to is the rule of thirds, which is where a composition is split into nine equal parts to form a three-by-three grid. Rather than place the main elements in the center of the picture, you would position them at one of the four intersections of the grid. This principle can also be used in your web page to focus attention on the key content.

You can also use grids to give your layouts more balance and structure. You can take that idea of a simple three-by-three grid, but it is probably more useful to break it down further into, say, twelve or sixteen columns. All elements on the page should then be sized to fit into the grid, all properly aligned with each other. Using a grid can make it much easier laying out your page and setting dimensions, but more importantly your design should be easier on the eye if everything is in proportion.

One of the dangers of using grids is that your design could end up looking a bit too rigid and boxy. To avoid this try not to put borders around all elements and soften things with a few curved edges, color gradients, and drop shadows in your design. You don't have to be a slave to the grid either, so don't be afraid to break up some of those straight lines with well-placed images for greater impact.

The 960 Grid System takes this design theory and provides templates, sketch paper, and CSS to help you set the dimensions of all the elements of your web page layout: 960.gs.

If the math is too much for you, try goldenratiocalculator.com.

The Sony Music website follows a clear grid structure with the Featured Artists content evenly spaced: www.sonymusic.com

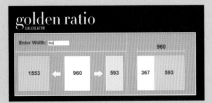

Screens that scroll

There are plenty of content slider plug-ins available, but bxslider.com offers one of the most flexible.

Pinterest.com allows endless scrolling, so a button to go back to the top of the page is crucial.

See mocoloco.com for a good example of horizontal scrolling.

As we have already established, there is nothing wrong with scrolling. We have all become very used to using the scroll bar to navigate the page and are unlikely to walk away just because what we are looking for is not immediately visible.

That isn't to say that you can't have too much scrolling—pages of endless text can seem like a marathon, especially on a small screen. But is it better to scroll or split big chunks of content into multiple pages? Very long pages will have a larger file size, which could therefore affect the time it takes to download, and search engine spiders might also give up before they scan the end of the document, meaning that some content might not get indexed. But breaking up content into chunks isn't always a good idea either—having to click for the next page requires a little more effort from the user than just continuing to scroll, and it presents an opportunity for people to give up reading any further.

A relatively new phenomenon is endless scrolling, where you might never reach the end of the web page because it is continuously adding more content the further you scroll down. You'll see this feature on some blogs and huge sites like Facebook, and it can be added to your pages using a JavaScript plug-in. Use with caution, however, because there are downsides; these pages can take up a lot of the computer's memory, which could result in noticeable performance issues; there is no facility to "remember" your position on the page if you navigate away from it; and the footer of the site may become redundant.

For particularly long or endless pages, it could be worth adding "back to top" links in the content so people don't have to scroll all the way back up to get to the navigation. You could even use a script to detect how far someone has scrolled and show a button if necessary, like on pinterest.com.

Some sites have even resorted to horizontal scrolling, like mocoloco.com. Although unconventional, it can actually feel more natural on touch-screen devices. Of course,

not all of us have an iPad yet, so perhaps it is not something you should try unless you are feeling particularly *avant-garde*.

Don't add scroll bars where people are not expecting them, such as on a box in the middle of the page. It might be tempting to add one where the content won't fit a section that you want to keep at an exact height, but resist if you can. This kind of scroll bar can be confusing, fiddly to use, and not particularly attractive. The exception is for text area input boxes, where you don't know how much text is going to be added.

An alternative way of scrolling is to use content sliders or carousels. Rather than have scroll bars, you have forward and back arrows to cycle through the content either horizontally or vertically. This slideshow effect can be set to run automatically, although you should still let the user control what they see.

Using tables

Mint.com shows that presenting data in tables doesn't have to look boring, and it makes good use of dynamic filters.

HTML tables were created to present tabular data, as you would expect, but until quite recently tables were also routinely used for designing page layouts.

Because you were able to remove the borders on the table, this enabled designers to create an invisible grid to help position their text and images. They ended up nesting tables within tables and using transparent spacer images to stop empty cells collapsing and breaking the whole layout.

The problem is that although you might be able to get things looking exactly as you want with a table layout, it is extremely inefficient. Pages take longer to load and it is far harder to maintain content and ensure consistency across a whole site, because you'd have to change every page if you wanted to tweak the design. The non-semantic structure also plays havoc with assistive devices and is not search-engine friendly.

Thankfully the world has moved on and most web designers have long accepted the joys of CSS and table-less layouts. But it is surprising how often HTML tables are still used by developers for layout, particularly for forms. If it's used sparingly and it makes things easier then it is perhaps no major sin, but really there is no excuse not to use CSS.

There is still a place for HTML tables, of course, and that is for their intended purpose. If you need to display tabular data, it is important that it is displayed clearly and is easy to read.

All the attributes of the table should be set in the CSS, including the widths, padding, and borders. The column headers should be clearly labeled and distinguished from the rest of the data. Any shading should offer sufficient contrast with the text and borders should not be too bold. Color is often used to highlight particular values—like red for high and green for low—but try to not to rely on color to relate the information being shown.

If you have long tables, it is often worth breaking them up into pages, displaying a limited number of rows each time. You could also shade alternate rows to help make the data more readable, although whether this really makes any difference is debatable.

You can make tables a bit more dynamic by using Javascript plug-ins to make the columns sortable, ordering the data from high to low and vice versa. Plug-ins can also help you add filters and search functionality to your tables.

Effective footers

You can get creative with your footer design as they have at www.empirevintage.com.au.

Your footer can display further information about your company, but there's no need for it to be boring! Ronihind.com makes

good use of illustration while www.liberty.co.uk uses the footer to highlight its latest tweets.

It's all too easy to forget about footers. You'll understandably want to make a big impact with your header, and you'll take the time to make your content engaging, but who notices what's at the bottom of the page, right? But footers are important and deserve as much love and attention as the rest of your design to make them as effective as possible.

Of course, the footer is a convenient place to put all the links to the kinds of things you don't necessarily want to clutter up your main navigation. It's here that most people will expect to find the copyright details, terms of service, privacy statements, and other legal information about the site. It is also common to see full contact details including any social media links, but you can even add content like customer testimonials or your "about us" details if you feel they don't need a whole page of their own.

If you are designing a page for a client, they will usually allow you a discreet credit and link back to your site in the footer. This all helps your search engine rankings and anyone who likes the site will hopefully get in touch to see if you can do something similar for them. Some purists might not consider it best practice, but it is something that you will see regularly.

Although it is still true that you'll want to keep the key content towards the top of the page, after scrolling and scanning the content the footer is often the last place your visitors will come to before they leave your site. To rein them back in, you can highlight recent blog posts, tweets, or links to new content.

Rather than have a separate sitemap page, many sites now list all their pages in the footer. Although this should never act as a substitute for your main navigation, it can help your

visitors find their way around your site if it is organized well. If you have too many pages to list, you can just promote the most important ones. Some sites will list Frequently Asked Questions or How Tos with links to the relevant content, although you could argue that your navigation should be clear enough to not need this extra signposting. At the very least you should include a link to the sitemap and any help pages.

Your footer may be hidden away at the bottom of the page, but that doesn't mean it has to be boring. Web designers are getting increasingly creative with their footer designs, with good use of color and illustrations to tie the whole page together. Because you don't have to worry so much about logos, adverts, search boxes, and the kinds of things you are expected to cram into the header, you have a bit more freedom to be artistic.

Dealing with adverts

Google's AdSense lets you earn money by displaying ads on your site. It won't make you a millionaire, but the service is simple to use and offers everything from text-based ads to videos of all sorts of shapes and sizes: www.google.co.uk/adsense.

The Internet Advertising Bureau provides many useful resources for website owners including guidelines, ad standards, and advice on how to get the most out of internet marketing: www.iabuk.net.

Ads rarely do anything for the aesthetics of a web page, but sometimes they are a necessary evil. If you are developing a site for a client, you might have no choice but to accommodate banners, text ads, or other ads, so you'll need to make sure they work with your page layout as best you can.

If the choice is yours, however, then think very carefully before allowing advertising on your site. We all could do with a little extra revenue, of course, but generally you'll need to have monster traffic to generate any significant income. Ads can really cheapen the way your site looks, affect page load times, and even drive people away if they are overdone.

Some ads are more tolerable than others. Thankfully we have seen a move away from pop-ups and interstitials—those really annoying ones that shove the ad right in the user's face—getting in the way of the content they are after. Banners, buttons, skyscrapers, and other image-based ads are more accepted, and people are well used to seeing Google's text-based ads.

Ads come in a variety of sizes, so check what dimensions you are going to need to fit in to your design. Banners tend to be placed in the header, alongside the logo, but some sites opt to put them right at the top of the page, completely outside of the container. Other adverts tend to live in the sidebar, out of the way of the main content.

If you have any control over what is shown, try to make sure any ad is not too incongruous in terms of content or design. Also try to limit the number of adverts on the page, especially if they are animated—too much movement in different places can be very distracting.

Bear in mind that a significant number of users will use some kind of ad-blocking plug-in on their browsers. It's worth installing one yourself to see what your layout looks like when it is activated. Will the layout be retained as you want it once that advertising image has been removed? Will there be an odd-looking white space where there was once a banner? Some of these ad blockers will work by scanning for the word "ad" and so on, so to avoid elements being blocked try not to use words like this in your code or file names.

There are various ad-serving companies that'll pay you if they can dish up ads on your site. You'll usually have to have quite a high level of traffic before they will bother doing business with you and will often only pay on a "per click" basis. You might also need to go through a rigorous auditing process to make sure they only cough up for genuine traffic.

Designing for mobile devices

As mentioned earlier, mediaqueri.es features great examples of adaptive web design, such as these layouts for Food Sense: foodsense.is.

Mobify is a service that helps you easily create a mobile version of your site, particularly if you need it to support ecommerce: www.mobify.com.

Food Sense

75

Gone are the days when we had to be sitting at a desk to go online. We are now just as likely to be on a train, on the sofa, or even at the top of mountain when we access the web, and we are routinely using an ever-increasing variety of mobile devices. You'll want your website to cater for this significant and growing audience, so what do you need to consider?

The most obvious issue is that many mobile devices will have much smaller screens. Although most modern smartphones will be able to display any site on their web browser, you will often need to zoom in and pan around the page to actually see anything. This is fine for some sites, particularly if it's one you already know your way around, but it'd all be a lot easier if the whole page just fitted your screen.

Performance can also be an issue for mobile devices, because we often can't get the kind of broadband speeds we enjoy on our desktops. Although we are supposed to have widespread 3G coverage, there are plenty of times when we have to make do with GPRS, and such slow connections can make browsing some sites a real chore as you wait to download bloated scripts and giant images.

Another consideration is that mobile data charges can still be quite high, especially when roaming on networks abroad, so keeping file sizes low is very important to keep the costs down.

To serve the needs of mobile users you'll often see a completely separate version of a site, specifically optimized for the small screen. This mobile version will have its own domain,

but users can be automatically redirected if a mobile user is detected. Detection of mobile devices can be accomplished by either server or client-side script, although neither method is 100% foolproof.

Mobile versions are usually designed to be more lightweight and so might use smaller, fewer, or no images at all, and will dispense with any dynamic elements. The layout will be simplified, but often so will the content—you might not be able to get the same level of information as on the full version of the site.

Creating mobile sites like this is not necessarily a bad thing, but could mean that you have to maintain two different versions of your site, and users might get confused if they can't use the site as they would expect.

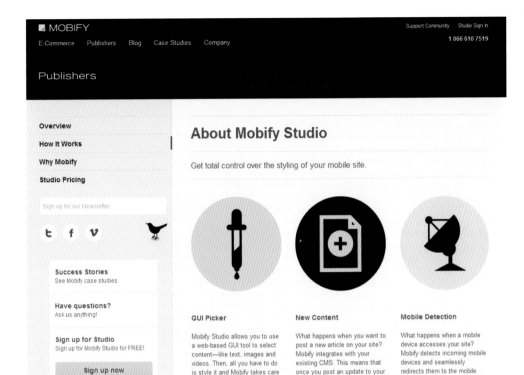

If you do go down this route, always give people the option to use your normal site instead and make it clear that a mobile version is available on your main site.

An easier way to cater for mobile users is to create a mobile style sheet for your standard site that will overrule your main styles when a mobile visitor is detected. You can change the formatting for your mobile style sheet to something that might be more appropriate for a small screen. You'll want to avoid horizontal scrolling, so you should set a narrower page width and change to a single column layout. You can remove large background images or call up smaller versions to reduce page sizes.

Remember that people will be using their finger to navigate your pages rather than a mouse, so hover-over effects might not work so well. You should also make navigation items large and simple to use, as those of us with fat thumbs get very frustrated when we can't click on the right link.

Mobile devices now come in all shapes and sizes and have different capabilities, so even if your mobile style sheet displays nicely on one it might not work so well on another. But as we have mentioned already, the @media query lets you serve up the appropriate layouts for each device. This means you can create a page with a width of 320px designed to look perfect on an iPhone and set another rule that caters for the larger screen of an iPad.

Now that we are increasingly using a variety of devices to access the internet, this kind of responsive web design has become much more widespread. But don't forget that not everyone will have the latest smartphones that support CSS3 and other technologies. Test your site on as many mobile devices as you can or with emulators that are available from device manufacturers and platform providers like Apple, Google, and Blackberry.

Look good in print

printfriendly
Save Money & the Environment

Browser Tool   Website Button   Support

Make any web page print friendly

http://www.mashable.com   print preview

Try it: CNN, Wikipedia, Mashable, ESPN

Get the **Bookmarklet**

Add Print Friendly to your browser.

Print Friendly

Drag the button above to your browser's bookmark toolbar.

Instructions

Get the button for your website!

Print Friendly

get your button

How it **works**

If you are feeling a bit lazy, you can use a service that adds a "print friendly" button to your pages linking to a print-optimized page, which can then be saved as a PDF or emailed: www.printfriendly.com.

For documents like event tickets and gift vouchers, it is often necessary to export to PDF before printing. Not only will this ensure that the design prints out as intended and can be properly validated, but it will also mean people can save the document to print out when required.

We often forget about how web pages might look when they are printed, but there are plenty of circumstances when it is essential. Sometimes it's not always practical or even possible to go online, and you might need to print out notes for a meeting, directions for a car journey, or even tickets for a concert. Just as you can specify different style sheets for mobile devices, you can create a CSS file that the browser will know to use whenever someone prints a web page.

When someone prints off your page they usually just want to see the main content, so there are some elements that they will not need. You can set the print.css to not display the navigation, for example, or remove a sidebar. Things like search boxes and login buttons are also unnecessary, and perhaps even icons and other images can be ditched. Everything will also have to fit nicely on a sheet of 8.5-x-11-inch paper—there is nothing more annoying than a having vital words chopped off a page you have printed. You can use the page-break CSS property to specify this explicitly if required.

Obviously people can't follow links on a printed document, so you can remove any coloring or underlining on these. It is possible to use a bit of CSS wizardry to display the URL in brackets after the link, so people can refer back to it as necessary, but this won't work on every browser.

There's a good chance that people are not printing in color, so it's worth ensuring that all text is black and the backgrounds are white, or at least that they have a significant enough contrast. You might also want to play around with font sizes and styles—serif fonts are considered better for printed material, for example. Basically you need to make the styles as simple as possible, so people can print your pages quickly and save valuable ink.

Many sites will provide a link to the print-optimized page so people can preview it before printing, but this is not essential. Just make sure you print it out yourself, in black and white, to check that everything is appearing as it should.

Chapter 6
Look and Feel

Choosing a design theme

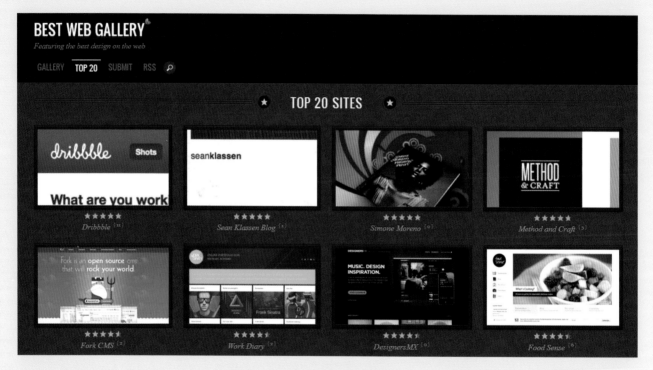

BEST WEB GALLERY
Featuring the best design on the web

GALLERY   **TOP 20**   SUBMIT   RSS

★ **TOP 20 SITES** ★

★★★★★
Dribbble [11]

★★★★★
Sean Klassen Blog [8]

★★★★★
Simone Moreno [9]

★★★★★
Method and Craft [3]

★★★★☆
Fork CMS [2]

★★★★☆
Work Diary [2]

★★★★☆
DesignersMX [0]

★★★★☆
Food Sense [6]

Get inspiration from web design galleries like bestwebgallery.com.

Picking a design theme can be the most difficult decision you have to make when building your website. You need to consider the typography, color, layout, and images you'll use, and all these elements have to work well in harmony with each other to get the look and feel you want.

You need a design that is appropriate for the subject matter and the audience you are trying to reach. Sometimes this is obvious—pastel colors and cartoon images might work well for a baking site, but less so for a law firm—but you should have done your research to find out what your visitors expect.

Take some time to have a look around the web to see if there is anything that catches your eye. You can get a feel for the latest trends by following web design blogs like smashingmagazine.com, but don't get sucked into trying to be too cool for your own good. It's not always easy trying to replicate what the top pros can achieve, and you need to focus on what is right for you.

Before you start to actually build your site, mock it up first. Sketch it out on paper initially, then try to create some draft designs in your favorite graphics package. Play around with different layouts, colors, fonts, and images to see what works—it's well worth sharing your ideas with others to get a second opinion.

Some aspects of your design might be set in stone already. Established organizations could have a recognized brand identity that is used across all media, so you might be limited in what you can do. This isn't necessarily a bad thing, as it gives you a solid starting point to build on.

Although it is good to think about your design before you begin writing any code, you don't have to get everything perfect the first time. If you use your style sheets well, it should be pretty easy to change most elements as you go along without too much pain. But don't get locked into an endless cycle of tweaking your theme—it is better to make up your mind early and focus on the content.

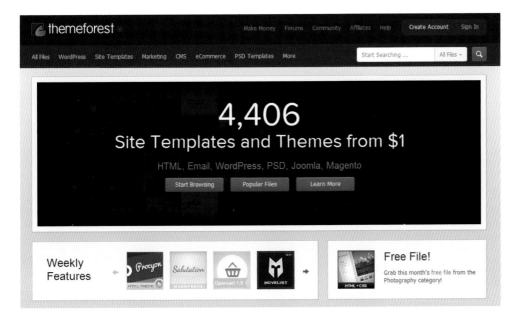

If you are prepared to pay a few dollars for someone to do the hard work for you, take a look at the ready-made design themes at themeforest.net.

Choosing colors

Color Scheme Designer is an excellent tool that helps you select a suitable palette for your website, even providing example pages based on the colors selected: colorschemedesigner.com. Equally useful is Adobe Kuler, which let's you create your own palette and view those of others: kuler.adobe.com

The colors you choose probably have the biggest impact on the overall look and feel of your website. A good palette can help make your website look warm and welcoming, but get it wrong and the same pages can look cold and boring.

We all respond to color in different ways, so think about your target audience when choosing your color scheme. Younger people might appreciate vivid colors more than older visitors, and women often prefer softer colors than men. Also consider the meanings associated with particular colors—for red it could be passion, excitement, or even danger, while green is usually thought more restful, signifying nature or health. Remember too that that each color might mean different things to different nationalities and cultures, so do your research carefully to avoid negative connotations.

Don't overdo the number of colors you have on the page—five should be the maximum—and take care that they complement each other. The way you combine colors is particularly important for people with visual impairments. Make sure that there is enough contrast between foreground and background colors so that text can be read more easily. Some combinations are particularly difficult for people with color blindness, such as red and green or blue and yellow.

You should also try not to convey information with color alone. Links, for example, should not just be a different color but distinguished with underlining or bold formatting. Check what your pages look like in black and white to make sure everything is still readable. The easiest way to do this is to print your pages out on a grayscale setting or use the service at graybit.com.

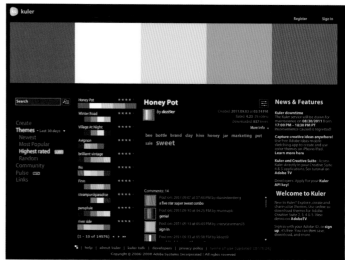

Web colors are usually specified with hex value, where #000000 is black and #ffffff is white. There are also names for colors in CSS, and you can use RGB values too, but it can be more efficient just to use hex values.

You should only use your CSS to specify colors, and if you specify one element you should specify all to make sure your pages look the same for everybody. That being said, not everyone will see your colors in exactly the same way. There will be differences in the way different browsers display specific colors, and everyone who visits your page will have their screens set up differently too. Bear this in mind if you are putting images such as logos on colored backgrounds, as the colors might not match as well as you think they do—use transparent GIFs or PNGs to make sure the image blends in properly.

If you're not convinced that you know which colors go well together, you can take a look at what other people have done. Sites like kuler.adobe.com and www.colourlovers.com show you the latest trends and offer a wide variety of color palettes that you can use on your own site.

ColorZilla is a handy Firefox add-on that gives you a color picker and lets you analyze the colors used by a particular webpage.

If you want to know what colors go best with your logo or what will complement your main photo, you can simply upload your image to Pictaculous and it'll suggest a suitable palette: www.pictaculous.com.

The typography challenge

Typography is important. Whether it is in print or on screen, the fonts you select and the way you use them contribute greatly to the overall look and feel of your design. Text needs to be clear and easy to read, of course, but different typefaces are appropriate for different audiences and the mood you are trying to convey.

There are thousands of fonts to choose from, but why do we see the same old few used across the web? The problem is that we don't all have the same fonts installed on our machines, so what looks fine to one person might not work for others. That's why "web-safe" fonts like Arial, Verdana, and Georgia have become ubiquitous online, because they can be viewed by all. But it doesn't have to be that way—there are many techniques to allow you to use any font you like on your pages, to help you make your website stand out from the crowd.

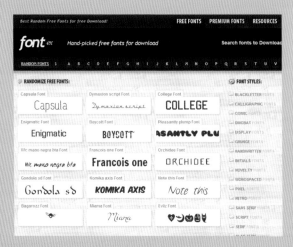

"Web-safe" fonts. Others include Impact and Lucida Sans (sans serifs), and Times New Roman and Palatino Linotype (serifs).

Check out resources like www.fontex.org for a huge range of free fonts available for download.

CSS2 introduced the @font-face rule that allows you to embed fonts in your web page. It is simple to use—just add the font file to your web directory and reference it in your CSS code. A slight complication is that different browsers support different font formats, so you need to provide different code and files to cater for each one. If that seems like a challenge, you can use tools that generate all the CSS and file formats for you—try www.fontsquirrel.com.

Unsurprisingly, commercial font foundries have a few concerns about font embedding as they often place strict conditions on the use of their fonts. These restrictions could be a serious barrier to improving web typography, but thankfully you will be able to find thousands of free fonts to use without any licensing concerns—www.fontex.org is a great place to start looking.

Once you have selected your typeface, you can specify the font size, color, and other properties in the CSS for each element. You have a surprising amount of control over how your text looks, making the most normal of fonts appear more interesting by playing around with the letter spacing, font weight, line height, and other attributes. You can also create some great effects using CSS3's text-shadow, although note that not all browsers will support all attributes.

Spare a thought for people whose eyesight might not be as good as yours and make sure your text will be readable to all. Some fonts, particularly the more artistic or "handwritten" styles, do not scale well, and small fonts can look even smaller on large monitors. It's good practice to give fonts a relative rather than fixed size so people can zoom the text, but check what effect this will have on your overall layout.

CSS is not the only option for using non-standard fonts on your pages. Some designers might resort to images instead of actual text to get the look they want, but that can leave you with a whole heap of accessibility and usability issues. You can use an image replacement technique instead, where you retain the text but overlay it with an image displaying the same text in a different font. Alternatively, there is sIFR, which replaces text with Flash or Cufon, using JavaScript wizardry to convert your font files into something that can be seen on screen.

Each method has its pros and cons, but whichever you choose it will not be foolproof. You should always specify suitable fallback fonts to use if the one you want can't be displayed by the browser. These should include one of the web-safe fonts, but generic fonts like sans-serif or serif should be the last option.

Alistapart proves that you don't need fancy pictures to create a stylish website: www.alistapart.com.

Google has also muscled into the fonts market, offering loads of free typefaces specifically designed for the web. It even hosts the fonts on its server and provides the necessary code to use them on your site, so it couldn't be simpler: www.google.com/webfonts.

One of the issues with font-replacement techniques is that they are not necessarily instantaneous. Your visitors might initially see the "normal" text before the replacement font, script, or image has loaded, which can take something away from the initial impact of your design. This effect will be exacerbated the more you use replacement fonts, so it might be better to use web-safe fonts for body copy and only call up one or two font variations. You can use a script to delay the presentation of the text until the necessary files have loaded, and you can improve performance by ensuring that your files are compressed on the server.

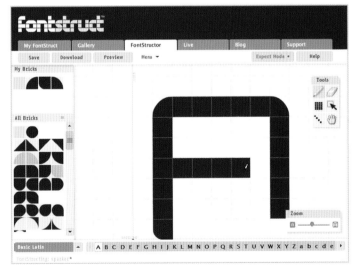

If you can't quite find the font you need, why not design your own? FontStruct (fontstruct. com) is a free font-building tool.

Using images

Choosing the right images for your website is extremely important. People will see the pictures before they read your words, so you want your images to make a positive impact on people as soon as they come to your site. A good image can lift the design and quickly communicate what the site is about, but choose poorly and you can make your pages look cheap, unappealing, and even confusing.

If you are selling luxury cars or showing off a holiday resort, then picking good-looking pictures should be pretty easy. If you are selling something less tangible, it can be

much more difficult choosing images that convey what you are offering. One solution is to use imagery that might imply a particular attribute of your business—water to mean clarity, or rocks to signify strength, for example. Try not to make the connection too obscure and don't use an image just for the sake of it. Focusing on good use of typography and color makes for a much better visual impact for your website than shoving in a bad photo.

There are many image libraries out there offering royalty-free content. This usually means that you still have pay, but you get a license to use the image as you want on your website. The

quality of these libraries can be patchy, and you'll have to wade through some pretty cheesy pictures to find what you need. Stock images are usually fairly affordable, but you'll undoubtedly find that the best ones are often the most expensive.

However tempting it may be, don't just do a Google image search and take whatever you find. The big stock libraries have become very adept at sniffing out sites that use their copyrighted images and are happy to send out scary letters and big bills. A better option is to try photo sharing sites like Flickr.com, where many photographers will let you use

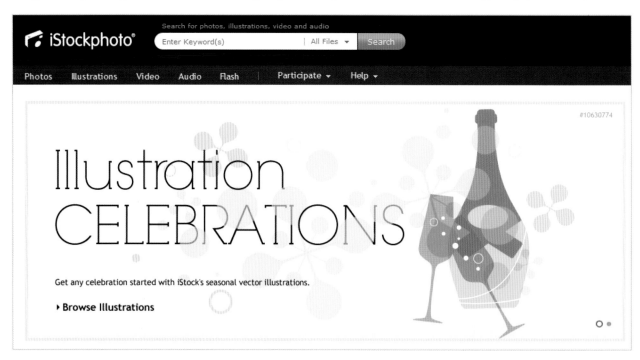

For a one-stop shop, www.istockphoto.com offers illustration, video, audio, and flash as well as photos. You buy a number of credits, which can then be used to download the files you need. The amount of credits depends on the size, complexity, and creator. The best feature is the ability to add potential pictures to a "lightbox," which you can share with others to help you decide which to buy.

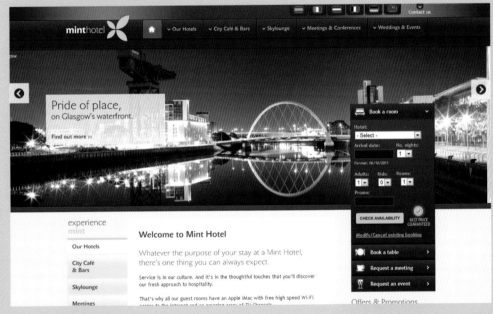

Mint Hotel, for example, has a simple but effective logo and makes great use of photography: www.minthotel.com.

their photos free of charge. Of course, the cheapest and easiest way to get what you want might be to take the photos and create the images yourself.

If you are designing your own logo, think about what you are trying to convey and keep it clear and simple. Using plain text with a good font is often much better than attempting to create something more abstract. Website logos will sit in the header, so design something that fits well in that space. Avoid too many colors and gradients, and consider the different backgrounds with which the logo will be used. Your logo says a lot about who you are, so it's important to get it right—it might be wise to get the experts in rather than attempt something yourself.

Make sure you optimize your images for the web and choose the appropriate format. JPEG images are usually best for photographs, but you need to compress them so that the file size is manageable but without an obvious drop in image quality. Logos and other graphics should be in GIF or PNG format—GIFs are often better for simple images, but use PNG where gradients or shadows are used because they support a much greater number of colors. Both formats offer transparency, but note that some older browsers do not support PNG transparency, though there are scripts available to fix this issue. Scalable Vector Graphics (SVG) is a text-based graphics language used to create vector images that can be zoomed or resized without any loss in quality. Although your images are described with XML, you'd usually create them with a graphics package such as Adobe Illustrator or the open-source Inkscape. SVG is compact, easily compressible, and supports scripting and animation. It is also an open standard agreed by the W3C, but despite these many advantages it has been held back by the lack of browser support, particularly from Internet Explorer.

Using backgrounds

Not so long ago, too many websites just looked like a rectangular sheet of A4 paper stuck in the middle of your monitor. Thankfully times have changed, and you'll now see more effective use of backgrounds to give pages greater warmth and depth.

Background images can be applied to the whole page to fill the screen with texture and color. You can use a single large image, but you'll need to make it wide enough to look effective at higher resolutions. Remember that the bigger the image, the larger the file size, so you might need to limit your background to the top of the page to improve performance. Alternatively, you can create a textured background from tiles, where a single small image is repeated seamlessly across and/or down the page, no matter what the resolution.

Don't let your background distract too much from the things you really want people to see. Many sites will use a separate plain background for the main content, making sure any text is easy to read and focusing the viewer's attention. Some sites will keep the background static while the content scrolls, although this is an effect that is tricky to get right.

Background images can be applied to any element you like and can often be seen on navigation bars, headings, and side panels.

A simple but effective technique is to add a subtle color gradient and a slight bevel to give things a "shiny" feel; you just need a small image (a single pixel wide) repeated horizontally.

You can also use backgrounds to make a more efficient use of images. For example, if your site uses many different icons for all the social media sharing options on your

The National Foundation for the Young Arts website uses video footage for the background. The clips are constantly changing and a menu allows you to scroll to different footage. The background becomes a static image when you navigate to one of the info pages. Check it out at www.youngarts.org.

There are plenty of free tileable backgrounds available, covering pretty much any effect you might need. Try www.textureking.com.

This Australian surf school has the perfect background while still keeping all the content clear: www.surfinparadise.com.au.

page, you can put these in a single file rather than save them all individually. You then just change the background position in the CSS to show the one you need. Using composite images like this will help your page load more quickly and give you fewer files to manage.

You are not limited to still images for backgrounds, although you have to be careful not to make your viewers feel too dizzy when they come to your site. Young Arts use video and photo backgrounds to great effect: www.youngarts.org.

Good use of background images can give your website the look of a glossy magazine, like they do at glo.msn.com.

Animation

Adobe's alternative design tool Edge can be previewed at labs. adobe.com/technologies/edge.

One thing that sets the web apart from publishing in print is that you can make things move. A bit of animation can liven up the dullest of content and give your web pages a much more dynamic feel.

The key thing to remember with animation is not to overdo it. While a single animated element can bring your page to life, two can split the viewer's focus and spoil the effect. If you have loads of things moving on the page, it might even make your visitors feel a little queasy.

Bear this in mind if you decide to run animated banners and other adverts on your site.Although they might bring in a little bit of revenue, they can be distracting and annoying for your visitors and can ruin your carefully crafted look and feel—you'll have to ask yourself whether they are really worth it.

Flash has always been the best-known and most used format for animations, despite it not being an agreed standard and requiring a browser plug-in to make it work. It is amazing what can be achieved with Flash if you know what you are doing, but you'll need the tools and skills to get the most out of it.

Although Flash has been the king of animation for a long time, you are now more likely to see animated effects created using CSS and JavaScript. You don't need special software, and you can even get away with limited artistic or coding ability—there are ready-made plug-ins from libraries like jQuery to help you create animated transitions, content sliders, menus, buttons, and much more.

If you want to be cutting-edge, you can use HTML5 and CSS3 to get things moving. Perhaps worried that Flash is quickly going out of fashion, Adobe is making the most of these new technologies to develop Edge

IMMERSIVE GARDEN
MOTION & INTERACTIVE DESIGNS

PROFILE
SKILLS
WORKS
ARCHIVE
CONTACT

Change perceptions and reach
the unconsciousness

It all started when I held a pencil
for the first time.
My name is Dilchan Arukatti and I am an
Art director based in Paris, experienced
in creating interactive and motion designs.
I am passionate about one thing,
creating outstanding pictures.

Feel free to contact me.

PROFILE

Immersive Garden shows
what the real pros can
do with Flash animation:
www.immersive-garden.com.

as an alternative animation design tool. Unfortunately, we are still some way from HTML5 being something that can be enjoyed by everyone on the web, but if you have one of the latest browsers take a look at labs. adobe.com/technologies/edge to see what is possible.

Although most people will be able to see Flash content, you should make sure that there is a suitable alternative where Flash is not detected. This can be a flat JPG image, but if you don't want people on devices like the iPad and iPhone to miss out on your animations, Google has developed a tool

that helps you convert Flash SWF files to HTML5 using the SVG format supported by all the latest browsers: www.google.com/doubleclick/studio/swiffy.

Although rarely seen in the wild these days, animated GIF images are also an option. You can use standard graphics software like Photoshop or GIMP to create your animations, but, with only 256 colors to play with and the need to create every individual frame, it can be difficult to get smooth and effective results.

SVG images can be animated too, using Sychronized Multimedia Integration Language

(SMIL). Despite the format being around for years with pretty decent browser support, it doesn't seem to have caught on. If you'd like to give it a try, check the resources and tutorials at carto.net.

Designing forms

People don't usually get too excited by forms, but the goal of many websites is to get people to sign-up for whatever information, products, or services you are offering. That means developing effective, clear, and simple ways of collecting information is often an essential part of your design and could be the difference between success and failure.

It should be obvious how to get to your form, what it is for, and why completing it is a good idea. Your users will want to get the whole process over and done with as quickly as possible, so only ask for the information you really need; it might tempting to get loads of personal information about your visitors, but this can be a real turn-off. The simpler the form, the more likely someone is to fill it out.

A common technique to help people focus on the questions being asked is to remove anything that might distract the user from the task at hand. This includes all navigation, adverts, and other escape routes.

Most people will assume all fields are required unless you say otherwise. Although it is common practice to mark required fields with an asterisk, it is better to use text or nothing at all. If you indicate that fields are optional, people are much less likely to bother filling them in.

You can place labels alongside, above, or even inside the fields, but they must clearly indicate exactly what information needs to be added where. If it is necessary to add more detailed descriptions of what is required, you can create tool tips that offer contextual help when you hover over a label or icon.

Services like www.wufoo.com help you create forms and surveys without getting your hands dirty with any coding.

All input fields should be a different color or have a border, but try not to add too much formatting. Fields should be an appropriate size for the expected text, and text areas should be used for longer comments—people should be able to see exactly what they are typing.

Use the right form elements for the right task: radio buttons should be used where exactly one choice is required from two or more options; checkboxes should be used

when someone can make any number or choices—including none—from a list of options; a single checkbox can be used for a single option that can be turned on or off; and drop-down selections can be used to make a single choice from a long list of options ("multi-select" drop-down menus should be avoided).

We know that most people instinctively navigate forms vertically, so avoid columns

Another form-building service is www.phpform.org. You can choose from a selection of themes, pick the types of menu you want, and edit the fields.

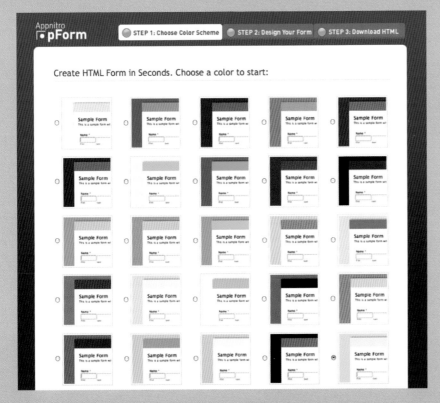

or putting fields side by side. If you have lots of questions you can group them into sections to make it more manageable, but try to keep your form to one page.

If people miss out or incorrectly enter information, make sure that the error message makes it clear what is wrong—don't just say "incorrect format" or something equally cryptic, but rather give a full explanation of the issue and what they need to do. You could highlight

where the problem is by making the fields bold and red, for example, but remember not to rely on color alone.

Adding forms to your site involves a bit more than design—there will be a bit of scripting and you'll probably need to collect all that information in a database. Wufoo provides a service that does all the hard work for you: www.wufoo.com.

HTML5 promises to do great things for forms by introducing new elements and attributes that should make their design more intuitive and improve the user experience. As ever, browser support is the stumbling block, so don't get carried away until you are sure what you are using is widely accepted

User customization

Allowing visitors to specify colors is helpful for people with visual impairments: www.bcab.org.uk.

iGoogle lets users choose from themes and widgets to customize their Google search page.

It is very tempting to offer your visitors the ability to customize the look and feel of your website to their own tastes, but you have to ask yourself whether it is really necessary.

You could let people adjust the fonts and colors, or even rearrange all the elements on the page, but you will have made all your design decisions for a reason—why let someone change your picture of perfection?

Adding user customization can actually make it more confusing for your visitor and distract them from the content you want them to see. If you are developing a complex web application that will require a degree of customer support, it is better that it uses exactly the same interface. Telling someone to look at the blue panel on the right is no good if they have changed all the colors and positions.

It is also questionable whether people even bother to use customization options when they are available. Your visitors should be

more interested in the information or products available on your site than the presentation, so it could all be wasted effort on your part.

User customization is more appropriate for accessibility, particularly if you are looking to cater for people with visual impairments. For example, you could add a facility that increases the font size of all text—although it might be argued that your visitors could easily achieve the same effect on any site by changing their browser settings. Another option is to allow people to change the color

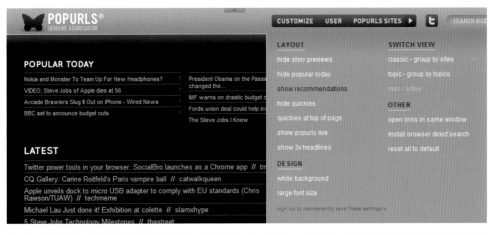

News aggregator Popurls.com offers a wide variety of customization options.

The BBC allows users to customize the site by choosing content topics of interest and color preferences.

contrast—so switching from dark text on a light background to light on dark—which some people might find easier to read. See the British Computer Association for the Blind at ww.bcab.org.uk.

Customized content also makes more sense for sites that offer a huge range of information that people are likely to come back to day after day. For example, if a daily news site offers business and sports sections, some people might be interested in one or the other, both, or neither, so you could let people choose

how and where that content appears. Perhaps the best-known example of user customization is iGoogle. It enables you to choose a "theme" for the Google search page and add "widgets" for all your favorite news and information, and then drag and drop these into your preferred layout.

If you do offer user customization, make it clear and simple to use and don't provide too many choices. You'll also need to test your site with every combination of options to make sure it still displays properly.

Chapter 7
Improving the User Experience

Don't make them think

Jakob Nielsen has been called the "King of Usability," although not everyone subscribes to his view of the web. His minimalist website might raise a few eyebrows, but you'll find some helpful advice: useit.com.

---

useit.com: usable information technology | Search |

useit.com: Jakob Nielsen's Website

Permanent Content

Alertbox
Jakob's column on Web usability

E-Commerce Usability (October 24)
Sites have improved, and we now know much more about e-tailing usability. Today, poor content is the main cause of user failure.

Mobile Content (October 10)
Mobile Usability Update (September 26)
How Long Do Users Stay? (September 12)

428 Alertbox columns from 1995 to 2011

Sign up for newsletter by email when a new Alertbox is published

Reports
Agile usability
Application design showcase: 10 best App UIs
Intranet usability
  › Intranet design annual
  › Enterprise 2.0
  › Intranet portals
  › Design guidelines for intranets, vols. 1-10
  › Intranet IA
  › Sector-specific: financial, government, tech
Email newsletters
E-commerce (13 vol. series) NEW and B2B sites

News

Usability Week 2011 Conference
  › London: November 13-18
  › Las Vegas: December 4-9

Full-day training courses, including
  › IA 1 (structure) & IA 2 (navigation)
  › Fundamental Guidelines for Web Usability
  › Mobile Sites & Touchscreen Apps
  › Visual Design for Mobile
  › Apps Design 1 (GUI) & Apps Design 2 (workflow)
  › Web Page Design & Emerging Design Patterns
  › Writing for the Web (2 days) & Writing for Mobile
  › The Human Mind: How Your Users Think
  › UX Basic Training

Tweets from past conferences

ClickZ Usability for Mobile Sites and Apps

uTest.com Testing the Limits

The Independent Website redesign: Why do we get so angry when the websites we love update their look?

Ironworks Video report from Usability Week San Francisco (2:34 min. video)

Once you have come up with a suitable design and layout, you'll want to concentrate on making the user experience as happy and painless as possible. And that isn't so much about making things pretty, as ensuring that your site is easy to use.

The key principle of good web usability is not to make your visitors think too hard. They should be focusing their attention on the content, not how they are supposed to navigate around your pages. When someone first visits your site they should instinctively know how it all works right away, and nothing should come as too much of a surprise. If they encounter a problem it should be clear what the issue is and how they can fix it. If they need assistance, help should easily be at hand.

It can be tempting to try to create something a little different from the rest of the crowd, but you have to be careful when flying in the face of conventional wisdom. Your visitors will be looking at hundreds of websites and most of them will work in a similar way: the navigation will be at the top or down the left-hand side, there will be two or three columns, links will be underlined, and so on. Once you start to deviate from the norm, people have to give things a little more thought. In some situations that might work well, but often it is just infuriating.

Usability specialists spend a lot of time looking at how people interact with websites, and their research has informed much of the industry's view on what is best practice—but web designers and usability experts don't

always see eye to eye. There is often a balancing act between what is beautiful and what is useful, and sometimes that means compromises need to be made on one side or the other.

Although some usability issues might be debatable, most of it is common sense. You are a user too, of course, and you'll know what you like and what drives you mad when you use the web. But if you aren't convinced by the arguments about how you should be doing things differently, the best thing to do is canvas opinion from others. You are not always the best judge of your own work, so put your site in front of others to see if the user experience really is as good as you think it is.

Effective links

Apache offers a guide to rewriting URLs to avoid overly long and meaningless addresses.

Avoid linking with phrases such as "click here" or "read on" and instead describe what you are linking to.

You should use relevant icons to indicate when you're linking to a document or media file that is not a web page.

Bad...

You can download our latest usability research paper here

Better!

2011 usability research paper

They way you use links is an extremely important part of the user experience. We all expect to be able to easily navigate our way around any site by using clearly labeled links, so getting this wrong will soon frustrate your visitors.

Links need to be obvious to everybody, so should be highlighted in a color that stands out from the rest of the text. The usual convention is to also underline links, but you'll see many sites that prefer to make the links bold to distinguish them instead, even though many usability experts would argue against that. Either way, the appearance of the link should change when you hover over it—by changing color or adding underlining—to reinforce the fact that it is clickable.

Do not underline headings unless they are links, because this could confuse people if

they try to click on it. Similarly, don't use the same formatting you are using for links to style other elements on the page.

Links should use text that describes what they are linking to and should work in isolation, so avoid using terms like "click here" or "read more." Keep the descriptions simple and to the point, but make it clear where the link will take them—visitors will only get annoyed if it is not what they were expecting. Do not use the same terms for different pages or different terms for the same page, and try to keep the link style consistent across your site.

You can link words within your content to highlight other parts of your site that people might want to go to, but don't over do it. Too many links can be overwhelming and make it more difficult to read the text.

Try to make it clear when you are linking to an external web page so people are not surprised when a completely different site appears. You can group these links under a heading, but otherwise use the URL or an icon to help distinguish them from the internal links on your pages. If you are linking to something

that is not a web page, like a PDF or Word document, you should use the appropriate icon. Email links should also be obvious so people know that their email software will be opened.

Create easy-to-read URLs for your pages to make it clear what each one is about. Addresses with long, meaningless query strings and numbers look ugly, but they are also less memorable and less likely to be used by others to link to specific content on your site. So an address like http://www.abc-widgets.com/top-widget is better than http://www.abc-widgets.com/prod/45/102040.php?cat=widg. If you use a content management system you should be able to change "permalinks" to give you pretty URLs, but otherwise you might need to set the URL rewriting on the server with .htaccess or IIS.

Effective links are not just something your users will appreciate, because search engines pay particular attention to them too. If your link text and URL contains the right keywords, your pages will be better ranked.

Creating meaningful error messages

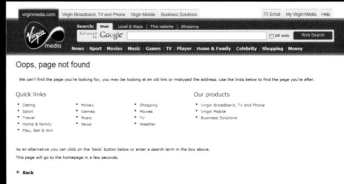

It's better to inform people why something hasn't worked, than using a generic invalid notification, and before they reach the end of an action, if possible.

"Oops, page not found" is much friendlier and more helpful to people than "error 404."

No matter how careful you are, things sometimes go wrong. You might make a typo in your code or forget to remove a link to a deleted page and not add the necessary redirect—or someone could simply mistype the URL. Rather than let your visitors be faced with the standard 404 File Not Found response, you'll want to give them something a little more useful.

You should create a custom error page that explains what has gone wrong and where they can go. This page should use broadly the same template as the rest of your site, but without too many distractions. Adding the navigation can be helpful, but make sure it is dynamically updated each time your site changes.

The language on your error page should be simple and brief, free from any technical jargon; "Error 404," for example, will be meaningless

to many people. Don't blame your user for the problem and help them find the content they need by providing a search box or link to a sitemap. You could also provide contact details, maybe asking that people report the problem to you so you can fix it as necessary.

Once you've created your custom error page and saved it as 404.html or similar, you'll need to tell the server to show it in the event that an error occurs. You can do that by adding a line to the .htaccess file or changing the IIS settings.

Although 404 errors are the most common, you can create custom pages for other types of errors such as 403 Forbidden or 500 Internal Error.

You might also need to provide error messages on the page, particularly when your users are completing forms. The same principles apply: tell people that there is

a problem, where and what that problem is, and what they need to do to fix it. The error should be highlighted clearly; red text is commonly used, but it is also good to use an icon or other visual signal. It is helpful to highlight specific issues as they occur rather than wait for a form to be submitted or action completed, although sometimes that might not be possible.

Hopefully the user interface and instructions you provide should keep user error to a minimum, but remember that your visitors might not be quite as switched on as you think. However obvious the problem might seem, keep your error messages friendly and apologetic and test them by making all the mistakes your visitors could feasibly make. You don't have to come up with a specific message for every eventuality, but you need to be confident that your users will not be left high and dry without a clue about what to do next.

Optimizing for speed

When we were all relying on 56k modems for our internet, optimizing your website for speed was essential. Having to wait a minute for a page to appear was a serious turn off, and some sites became practically unusable for those on a dial-up connection. As broadband became more ubiquitous, however, download speed was seen as less of an issue by many designers, and any people still stuck in the slow lane were often forgotten.

We should remember that even in these days of super-fast fiber optic connections, not everyone has broadband, and many of us still have to rely on shaky GPRS cell-phone signals while we're on the move. And even where we have decent bandwidth, plenty of sites are using so many huge images, style sheets, fonts, and scripts that we're often back to waiting too long for content to appear.

It's not just your visitors that will appreciate speedy downloads, as Google is now taking page speed into account in its search engine rankings too. Large page sizes will also put a greater burden on your web server, meaning you might be less able to cope with spikes in demand. It could even cost you more if you have data transfer limits on your hosting account.

The first thing you should do is to make your HTML, CSS, and JavaScript as lean and efficient as possible. Remove redundant code and don't call unnecessary external files when the page loads. Optimize all images using the appropriate formats and use image tiling and CSS sprites where appropriate.

To help speed up things further you should enable gzip compression and caching on your web server, both of which will involve editing the .htaccess file on Apache or amending IIS on Windows.

Gzip compression works by "zipping up" your files on the server, which are then sent to the web browser as they are requested, and then unzipped once they have been received. This simple process can make a huge difference to page speed, particularly if you are using JavaScript libraries and complex style sheets.

File caching is where the browser stores files locally so that they are not downloaded every time someone visits a new page on the same site. You can set the caching rules on the server so that the browser knows when it should check for new content. So for content that is unlikely to change often—like a PDF or image file—you'd set an expiry date or a maximum age of a year. For content that might change frequently, like HTML or php files, then it'd be something like a few hours.

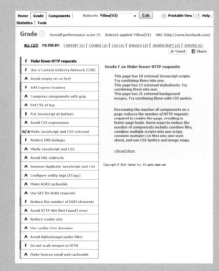

You can check how well your pages perform with services like Google's PageSpeed at developers.google.com/pagespeed and Yahoo!'s Yslow at developer.yahoo.com/yslow; both give detailed tips on how to make your pages faster.

Leaving users in control

One important rule of web usability is to always leave your users in control. You need to let people choose what they want to see and when then want to see it.

This is particularly important when thinking about the control of the web browser. For instance, the Back button is used extensively by all people navigating the web, so it should work exactly as they expect it to. And don't be tempted to use scripts that resize the browser window and change the appearance of toolbars and scrollbars—it is unnecessary and will just confuse and annoy your visitors.

One issue that sees a great deal of debate is whether you should open external links in a new browser window. Many site owners will say yes, because they don't want their visitors to leave their website, hoping that by keeping it open on another tab it will encourage people to return after they have looked at the external content.

But if someone follows an external link, they are choosing to leave your site and will expect to see a new page. If they want to return to your site, they are quite capable of using the Back button as necessary. If they want to open a link in a new tab, many of them will know exactly how to do that too.

There are exceptions: if the link is to something that isn't a web page, like a PDF document, then this should be opened in a new window. Another exception is when linking to a help page, where you don't want a user to be interrupted during a process, such as completing a form.

Don't provide content that your visitors have not requested. One annoying but all-too-common practice is to present a pop-up in the middle of the screen asking people "to complete a short survey about the site."

Avoid making audio and video files start automatically; instead, provide a clear play button and other controls to adjust the volume or resize the window.

Adverts are also something that can take control of a web page, preventing users from seeing the content until the ad closes or runs its course. If you want to run campaigns like this, ask yourself whether the extra revenue is worth the hindrance for your visitors.

Using pop-up windows

Urban Outfitters is a good example of where pop-up windows can work well—people can see a garment at a glance, clicking on particular links for further information: www.urbanoutfitters.com.

Popup Test puts your pop-up blocker software through the mill to see if it's up to scratch: www.popuptest.com.

Pop-up windows are created using JavaScript to open a new browser window, and you can control the size of that window, where it is positioned, and what controls the user sees.

You can even launch the new windows as soon as someone visits the page, but in the past that has led to them being hijacked by advertisers keen to push their products in front of a captive audience. It seemed that every time you went online you were bombarded with dozens of windows, which you hadn't asked for, trying to sell you all sorts of stuff you didn't need, and so the pop-up soon became the scourge of the web.

However, pop-up windows can be useful when you need to provide further information to your users but do not want them to leave the page, such as help boxes or terms and conditions when people are completing forms.

Even so, there are still some accessibility and usability issues with pop-up windows, and the content might not be indexed by search engines. But the real problem is that people got so fed up with their use for advertising —legitimate and otherwise—that most web browsers now come with some sort of pop-up blocking functionality. This means that they should be avoided wherever possible.

Old-school pop-ups might just about be dead, but they have risen in another form. Rather than opening up a new browser window, a better option is to use CSS and JavaScript to create "modal windows." In this case the content is still on the HTML page but hidden until the user clicks on the appropriate link. You have much greater freedom on how the pop-up is styled, and you can use techniques like fading out the rest of the page to help it stand out and focus the user's attention. A common use is to show

larger versions of images when you click on thumbnails. As ever, there are plenty of jQuery solutions to get the effect you need.

Care still needs to be taken when using modal windows, and you should make sure the user chooses the content and is not surprised to see a pop-up. It should be clear how the pop-up can be closed—usually an "X" in the top corner or a submit button—but it is now common practice to close the window if the user clicks anywhere outside the box.

Providing help

Check out edublogs.org to see
their range of video tutorials.

Visitors can receive live help
from a virtual sales assistant
at Rackspace.com.

The more you are willing to help your visitors, the more likely they are to give you their custom. Providing effective online help can also save you much time and money, as you can rely on your website to give people most of the answers they might need without needing to give you a call.

It is often a good idea to create a Frequently Asked Questions—or FAQ—page. This should clearly list the queries you commonly receive and provide comprehensive but simple-to-understand answers. If necessary, provide links to the relevant pages or screenshots to illustrate what they need to do. If you have lots of potential questions, break them down into broader subject areas so people can easily find the one they need and provide a keyword search facility.

You won't be able to answer every question in an FAQ, so always provide an email that people can use if they need further assistance. It is great if you can also provide telephone

helplines, but make it clear how much it is going to cost. Your customers will appreciate a toll number, but will be furious if you charge a dollar a minute.

Provide links to any relevant help at the appropriate places in your content. Rather than link to new pages, you could use tool tips or pop-up boxes that appear when you click on the help link or icon.

Some products and services will require tutorials to get people started, and these should be highlighted as soon as someone signs up. Take people through step by step using simple jargon-free language and annotated screenshots, although videos complete with audio commentary can be even better. Provide links to more detailed documentation, like PDFs of user manuals and any external sources of help, to ensure they have everything needed. Effective tutorials can save you a fortune in training costs and will encourage people to use more of your products.

Not every site needs to provide extra help to its visitors, because everything might already be obvious if you have good navigation and clear content. Don't provide FAQs and tutorials just for the sake of it. If everything really is simple to understand, then you could just come across as patronizing.

Software like Techsmith's Snagit is perfect for creating online tutorials and demonstrations, and your videos can be uploaded and shared with Screencast.com: www.techsmith.com/snagit.html.

If you have the manpower to spare, you can try a "live help" system. These let your visitors start a chat conversation with you or one of your representatives or request a call back, and they can be an effective way to boost sales.

Using cookies

Cookies are not always bad; they can be helpful too, such as when they are used to remember login details for frequently used sites.

Give your visitors the option to accept cookies or not and explain what they are being used for in your privacy policy page.

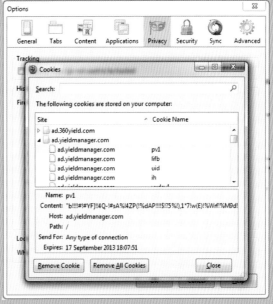

Web cookies have got a bad press. Many people assume that they are something evil to be blocked at all costs, whatever their purpose might be. Although it is true that they are used for nefarious purposes, cookies are often there to make things easier for people.

A cookie is just a simple text file that usually contains a website address and a unique ID. These can be generated on your server or by JavaScript so that they are downloaded to your visitor's computer when they first come to your site. This means that the user can be identified if and when they return to your site, and if necessary you can deliver content tailored to that person.

This can be very helpful if you need to login to use a particular website, for example. It can be annoying to keep having to enter your access details each time you visit, but if you accept a cookie then these details can be "remembered" by the website, making the process much easier. Cookies can also be used to store user preferences, keep items in shopping carts, track the user session,

and more—all of which are designed to improve the user experience.

Of course, it's not all good. Cookies are also used by advertisers looking to gather information about people and their preferences. This is usually perfectly legal, but it's not always clear exactly what details are being collected.

Although advertisers would argue that what they are doing is harmless, and is only to provide you with targeted adverts, many people are not comfortable with that. There is no doubt that cookies can be also used for more obviously insidious practices, and even innocent cookies can be hijacked to steal your details.

As a result, some people will set their web browsers to block some or all cookies, so your site should never rely on them for your pages to work. If you do set cookies, explain why you are doing so and, if possible, give your users the choice whether to accept them or not. Use your privacy policy page to highlight exactly what information is being collected by cookies.

If you are thinking of using cookies, there are various alternatives you should examine first. These include embedding information in the query string, hidden form fields, HTTP authentication, and JavaScript, although all have their own drawbacks and might only be suitable for certain circumstances.

Balancing security and usability

Offer a "Forgot password" function if your site requires users to sign-in, and, as with Skype, a username reminder can be helpful too.

Google shows an indicator of password strength to encourage people to be more secure.

We all know that online security is important, but it can also become a bit of a pain. Having to login and remember a password presents a barrier to the user, and it's not always one that is straightforward to overcome. Is it better to have a super-secure site that is hard to use or one that sacrifices some security to make life easier?

You have to consider how important security is to your users and that will depend on what lies behind the password—if the account were compromised, what is the worst that could happen? Would personal details be revealed? Would people have access to sensitive information?

It is obvious that services like online banking should have a high level of security, and you will usually see a two- or three-step process to login, often requiring a gadget that generates unique codes to use. But if logging in simply allows someone to post comments on a blog then security is not so much of an issue.

Most people understand why having a hard-to-crack password is important, but that doesn't stop many of them choosing the same simple word in lots of places. While it is always good to advise your users on what makes a good password, it can cause problems if you insist on particularly complex formats, such as requiring non-alpha numeric characters or at least one uppercase letter. Many people struggle to remember all their different passwords and end up writing the trickiest ones on a Post-It note or in a file handily called "passwords.doc" for any would-be laptop thieves to find.

One solution is to allow and encourage passphrases instead, maybe made up from separate words. Something like "dave likes oranges" is easier to remember and is probably more secure than "Orange5!" for example.

If you set passwords automatically, which are then sent by email—perhaps in a bid to prevent automated programs registering on your site—you should give users the opportunity to change them to something more memorable as soon as they log in. You should also provide a clear and simple "Forgot password" function that automatically sends the password to the registered email address.

Don't overcomplicate things. If you make it difficult for people to remember or retrieve their password, then people might not bother trying to log in at all.

User testing

Remote testing services like usabilla.com do the hard work for you at a resonable price, but bear in mind you can't choose your test subjects.

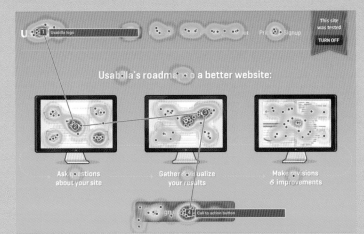

Ask questions about your site

Gather & visualize your results

Make revisions & improvements

ClickTale's mouse movement tracking service generates heat maps to show which content attracts the most attention, helping you work out what needs to go where for greatest effect: www.clicktale.com.

You might think your website is clear and simple to use, but your visitors may feel otherwise. Some kind of user testing is essential for making sure people will like what you are providing and will understand how it all works.

User testing is something that can be done at various stages of a website project—if you have an old site you are looking to replace, user testing can help identify what needs changing, and you can test mock ups and prototypes to make sure you are on the right track. You should definitely conduct some sort of user testing before you launch, but you can also canvas opinion after your website is live to make sure that it is still doing what it needs to.

The first thing you'll need is real people to give you some feedback. Ideally, these should be a diverse selection of users that reflect your likely audience. Existing users can be helpful, but it is also good to test your site with people who have no prior knowledge of your site. You

don't need to go overboard with your focus group; you'll need at least a couple of people, but five should give you enough feedback to work with.

Once you have your test subjects, you need to set them some simple tasks, such as purchasing a particular product or finding a specific document. You'll then need to watch how they use your pages and encourage them to talk about what they are doing. If you can, you should record them with a webcam and capture exactly what they are doing on screen so you can collate and review the results at a later date.

There is specialist software to help you, but you might not be able to afford full usability testing suites like Techsmith's Morae (www.techsmith.com/morae.html). If you are on a Mac, you can try the more affordable Silverback (silverbackapp.com), but really you can use any screen-capture software that supports audio and video.

Another option is to get someone to do all the testing for you. This used to be the domain of very expensive specialists, but now there are variety of affordable online remote testing services like usabilla.com, usertesting.com, and whatusersdo.com. The only drawback is that you might not have much control over what users are selected or have the opportunity to question them directly.

Chapter 8
Customer Processes

Registration

Registration for *The New Scientist* is kept simple and the use of a "captcha" deters spam bots.

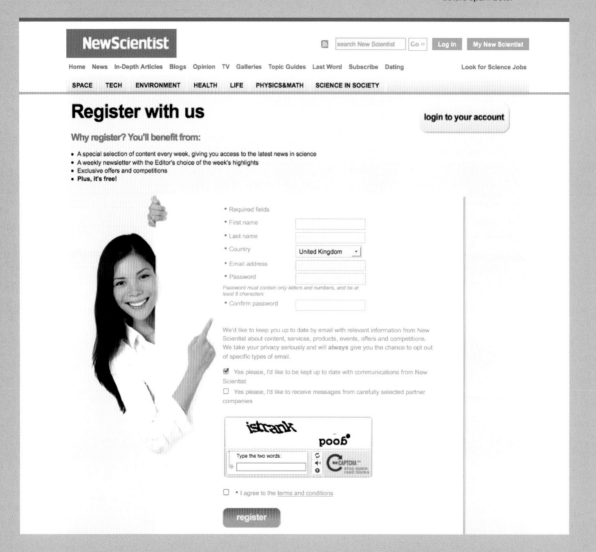

We're all familiar with the process of registering with websites before we are able to make transactions, join in with communities, or access premium content. Whether we are visiting a small online start-up or a huge brand like Amazon, it's likely that we'll have to provide a degree of personal information in return for a login and password that allows us to get to the information and services we came for. But adding a registration step to the visitor experience is actually quite a big decision for any site developer, because it presents disadvantages as well as advantages.

Can you remember a time when the additional step of registration has actually put you off the idea of using a site at all? Have you rejected joining a web service simply because of the inconvenience of that extra step to register?

If so, it's worth asking yourself why that was and trying to remove those obstacles for your own visitors.

Some people are put off by providing you with contact details. They might just find it a bit of a hassle, but might also fear an avalanche of spam and targeted advertising. Worse still, they simply don't trust your site will protect their personal information. It pays to make the process painless and allay any concerns potential visitors may have.

You should make registration as simple and easy as possible. It might be tempting to ask for loads of personal data, but you are increasing the chance of turning people away. Make it as basic as you can to begin with—you can always add fields later on, but in those early stages it's much better that your visitors tell others how simple registration is at your site, rather than how cumbersome it is. As for spam anxiety, head that off by asserting plainly that information will never be used by third parties, pointing people to your privacy policy.

The good thing about registration is that it allows you to capture an audience and their data. Email addresses and phone numbers in particular enable you to contact willing registrants with news, marketing, and special offers to entice them back to your site. Richer details enable you to target specific offers or services that individual visitors might find irresistible, or you could tailor content to suit them. Registration can also help you make money directly as your site matures by charging for membership benefits or premium content.

Don't demand registration too early in your business timeline or too early into each user's visit. They need to taste your wares before they sign up. Make password and login selection easy while trying to keep things secure. Email confirmation can be used to prevent visitors providing false contact information and to foil automated bots.

Building an online store

It's a good idea to make the "shop window" of your online storefront seasonal.

It might sound obvious, but highlight any special offers and make it easy for customers to take advantage of these.

Selling your wares online is not all that different from setting up a brick-and-mortar store. People won't be tempted to come in and browse if your storefront doesn't look attractive and professional, and they won't make a purchase if they can't find what they want.

Just like a conventional store window, your website's homepage should be used to highlight new and popular products and the latest special offers. It is a good idea to make these seasonal or linked to recent news stories if you can, but most of all you'll want to make these look as interesting and enticing as possible. Some things are easier to sell than others, so choose items with the biggest "wow" factor—whether that is something using the very latest technology, offering the most impressive savings, or simply the most attractive product.

The way you organize your store is extremely important if you want people to find what they are looking for. Categorize your products logically and clearly, giving each category its own page with search-engine friendly titles and URLs. If necessary, these can be broken down further into subcategories or maybe pages for different brands. If you have lots of products on offer it can also be helpful to add a search facility or filters for things like price or size to help prevent people having to go through dozens of pages to get to the item they need. The ability to sort products by price or popularity is also a feature that will be welcomed by many.

Use images that clearly show what the product looks like so your customers know what they are getting. For many products, particularly items like clothing and electronic equipment, you can't get away with just a thumbnail. As well as a decent-sized detailed picture you might need photos taken from different angles or in the full variety of colors available. Some shops will even let you zoom in and rotate the image so you can see every nook and cranny before you buy.

Provide detailed descriptions of every item, including facts like dimensions and exactly what the package includes. Not only will this make people more confident about their purchase, you're much less likely to get returns or complaints because something ordered is not as expected. Link to related products or necessary accessories so people don't have to go looking elsewhere—this is helpful for your customers, but might also boost your sales.

If you are confident in your coding skills, you can build your online shop from scratch and integrate all the necessary payment processing options within your design. But the easy option is to use out-of-the-box software that already has all the kinds of features you could possibly need. There are free open-source packages like osCommerce (www.oscommerce.com) and Magento Community Edition (www. magentocommerce.com), and ecommerce plug-ins are available for most content management systems. Alternatively you can pay for enterprise solutions or hosted web services like Actinic Online (actinic.co.uk).

Although much of the hard work will be done for you if you choose a third-party solution, you'll still need to consider many of the issues outlined in this book when building your storefront. You might also find that you don't have the kind of flexibility with the design or functionality that you need, which could be a problem if your site is more than just an online store. You will often see some organizations create a separate site for their ecommerce activities—not ideal, but if you do go down this route try to make the look and feel as consistent as you can with clear links between the two sites.

Hosted web services like Actinic Online (actinic.co.uk) offer ready-made ecommerce features.

Allow customers to refine their search and sort items by price or popularity.

Signposting the whole process

At picture-framing.co.uk you can customize your order to your exact requirements, and it does a great job at leading you through the process and showing you what you are doing.

Transactional websites can be complicated affairs for visitors, whether they are simply responding to a survey, filing a tax return, or conducting their weekly shop. In the same way that you can get lost and confused sitting in front of a pile of paperwork or dashing through the aisles of your local grocery store, your site visitors can get lost between pages 6 and 7, or between organic foods and bleach.

It's best to do what you can to keep them on the straight and narrow when possible. Clear, intuitive site navigation is an obvious help, but even great navigation can benefit from a little extra signposting to show visitors how to continue their journey or retrace their route.

Signposts are always a good place to start. Just as in the real world, stumbling across a signpost during a complex journey is very reassuring. Online, signposts can be used to direct different types of users to the areas

of your site they are seeking. Want to checkout now? Click this button. Don't know what this term means? Follow this link. Regardless of what you need your signposts to do, make sure they are visual, obvious, and link to the right place. Signposts make user journeys more accurate and speedier, which means they can buy your products and services quicker.

Breadcrumb trails are useful on shopping sites, but particularly helpful when filling in long forms, completing extensive applications, or just entering a lot of information across multiple branching screens for whatever you are trying to achieve. Just like the breadcrumbs of fairy tales, they lead you safely back where you have been to check you made the right decisions along your journey.

A variation of this is to not only show where your users have been, but to indicate what steps they have yet to complete. This means

they know exactly where they are in the process and what they can expect next. It's important when there are many stages to complete, but remember that if you make it look like there is a long way to go, they might not bother going past step one.

So make it clear at every stage what your users are doing, what they have done, and what is left to do—whether that is entering their bank details, selecting preferences, choosing delivery options, or making a payment. If people are parting with their cash, you must give them the opportunity to review their order and go back to correct any mistakes before it is confirmed.

Good signposting gives your visitors more confidence when going through any process and should make it more likely that they click that all-important button to confirm a sale or submit the information you want.

Completing the process later

Services like Formstack
(www.formstack.com) offer
forms with save-for-later
functionality built in.

Amazon allows you to create
a "wishlist" which you can
return to at a later date. Others
can even add to your list or buy
something on your behalf.

Your site visitors will always appreciate seamless features that make their experience that much more enjoyable, especially if they are perfectly in tune with their evolving browsing habits. On average, we all spend longer interacting with web services these days.

Instead of merely visiting a site, buying an item we want, and then logging out, we tend to browse, see what else is available, read detailed descriptions and reviews, and evaluate our options at leisure. Outside of ecommerce, we're now also far more likely to use rich web services to complete lengthier, more complex processes. Instead of downloading and printing a tax return, for example, we increasingly feel confident enough to complete it online.

However, modern life remains as busy as ever and finding a window in which we know we will definitely be able to start and finish these longer processes can be tricky. Nobody wants

to spend an hour carefully placing items in a shopping cart or calculating figures to enter into a loan application if there is even the slightest chance that the process will somehow get interrupted or time out, leaving no option but to start the whole thing again.

All leading ecommerce sites like Amazon, Dell, Nike, or Gap have some kind of "save for later" functionality with their shopping carts. Many of us will spend a long time thinking about and tinkering with our orders, leaving our Amazon shopping cart in limbo for hours while we slowly progress to the order to ensure free shipping.

In fact, with Amazon it's even possible to leave an open "wishlist" (www.amazon.com/gp/registry/wishlist), which anyone can visit to add and pay for items on your behalf.

Save-for-later functionality is available with most shopping cart services that you might

use for your site, but the ability to return to an online process isn't only desirable in an ecommerce environment. Any web form that requires multiple steps and spans many pages will also benefit from this kind of functionality.

Session cookies can be used to make forms more fault-tolerant and prevent users from getting frustrated at having to start all over again if they are forced to navigate away for whatever reason.

Inexpensive PHP and AJAX forms packages can be bought and bolted onto any existing design to help you add robust, cached form functionality without any specialist skills. Services like Formstack (www.formstack.com) and FormAssembly (www.formassembly.com) enable you to easily include complex surveys and forms that offer the option to let users save their progress and resume filling it in when they're ready.

Providing contact details

Dealing with queries from customers takes time and money, of course, so it is perhaps understandable why some websites will push their visitors to the online help rather than a phone. But that isn't going to work for everybody, and sometimes a question can only be answered with a call or email.

You should provide a link to a "Contact us" page on your main navigation, and this page should include all the necessary contact points. Companies and other organizations are often required to provide a telephone number and postal address as well as an email address, so check the appropriate legislation for your region. If you have different contact points for different branches or departments, make sure all are clearly labeled so people know which one they should use.

If you really want your customers to drop you a line, you can highlight your contact details prominently in your header or in the relevant places in your content.

If you want people to come to your real-world location then provide a map and any necessary directions. This could just be an image, but a better option is to embed a Google map into your pages.

Many sites will ask the people to use contact forms to get in touch with them, but think carefully before you go down this route. Forms can a be a real turn-off, and many people are more comfortable sending an email or making a phone call, so always provide alternatives to the form.

Contact forms can be more useful if you receive a lot of correspondence, because you can ask specific questions that will help you filter the messages. But the more questions you ask, the less likely people will answer them.

One of the reasons websites choose to use contact forms is to avoid receiving loads of junk by email, but forms are also attacked by automated robots that will try to send you lots of spam. Most decent contact form scripts and content management system plugins—such as www.fastsecurecontactform.com—will come with some kind of anti-spam security like a captcha, but remember that this is yet another hurdle someone has to jump before getting in touch with you.

If you are worried about your email address being harvested for spam purposes, there are various obfuscation techniques that foil some robots while still working normally for your visitors.

Finally, don't forget the small print. Provide visitors with your company number and registered address if you operate a limited company, and don't forget to make any necessary tax information easy to find, perhaps in the same footer as any business disclaimers you'd like to make.

It's all in the name: www.fastsecurecontactform.com offers contact form plugins for WordPress or PHP that come with anti-spam features.

You can embed a Google map on your contact page to encourage people to your real-world location, as seen on www.groundwork.org.uk.

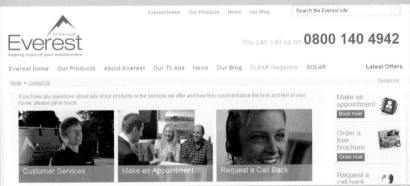

Everest let customers know they can get in touch by displaying their phone number prominently at the top of the homepage: www.everest.co.uk.

Payment options

If you want to make money by providing products, services, or information online, you're going to need to choose a payment system for your website. Although some businesses still insist on mailed checks or even cash-on-delivery, any ecommerce site looking to make revenue needs to accept online payments.

The first and greatest consideration when choosing a payment option must be security, both for your visitors and for your own business. Online transactions thrive on trust, and this can only be engendered through the peace of mind of a tried-and-tested secure online payment system that protects buyer and seller from the point of purchase, via full invoicing, through to receiving goods or services.

Setting up a merchant account online can be a similar process to adding an account that allows brick-and-mortar businesses to accept payments by credit or debit card. If you already have a merchant account offline, it's probably simplest to just get in touch with your bank and arrange to extend the service online—they'll be only too happy to help you get up and running, and you'll already have financial clearance, which will make the process quicker. If you don't already have such an arrangement, you can still setup an internet merchant account (IMA) through most of the best-known major banks. Typically this will cost you an initial fee plus a daily fixed fee or percentage charge on credit card transactions.

A payment processing gateway typically protects yourself and your customers from internet fraud by guarding card details as they pass from the customer to your merchant account, and then on to the payment processor that handles your back-end transactions. When a customer submits an order of any kind, that information is secured and sent to your web server through SSL (secure socket layer) encryption. SSL is also employed between your business and the payment gateway for your acquiring bank, which then handles processing with card issuers such as Visa, American Express, or similar. The card issuer then hopefully authorizes the request, returns the response back through the payment gateway, and then on to your site, which processes the transaction and closes the secure transactional loop. The whole thing takes seconds in real time.

PayPal dominates the online payment marketplace, enabling buyers with registered and verified bank accounts to easily transfer funds to online merchants. PayPal for Business also allows you to accept credit cards and invoice your clients. It is simple to set up and can be intuitively and quickly integrated into most site designs and with the majority of shopping carts. Perhaps its greatest strengths are that it is a recognized and trusted brand and that you don't need a merchant account. Many people will already have an account too, so they won't need to add all their details every time they buy. There are still fees, of course, but one drawback is the time it can take for funds to clear your business account (often four working days). Also, you might not get quite so much control and support as with other providers, and some online buyers simply refuse to use PayPal due to past experience and prefer a bank-powered merchant account.

Google's Checkout service is looking to compete with the likes of PayPal, and people can use their Google Wallet to pay for goods on a variety of sites. There are lots of ways Checkout can be integrated into your site, and it offers plenty of security and privacy assurances, a fraud prevention tool, and a rigorous Payment Guarantee. The downsides are similar to those associated with PayPal, but some visitors still get confused when asked to make a payment through a Google account. See checkout. google.com for more information.

Ultimately, if you want to add payments to your site, you've never had so many secure, trusted options. All ecommerce services and software will come with a selection of options that they support, which may include PayPal and Google as well as other well-known online transaction specialists such as WorldPay, Nochex, or PayPoint. If you'd rather skip the middleman and get a direct merchant account instead, then familiar banking brands such as HSBC now routinely support internet businesses.

Google checkout 🛒

| Home | What is Google Checkout? | How to use Google Checkout | How to Integrate | Help & FAQ |

How to integrate > **Buy Now buttons**

Offer Google Checkout in minutes with Buy Now buttons

If you don't offer shopping cart functionality on your website, you can start increasing your sales and processing them within minutes when you use Buy Now buttons. Just place the Buy Now buttons by items you sell on your site and buyers who click these buttons will be directed to a Google Checkout-hosted purchase page where they complete their purchase with Checkout. For digital goods, buyers will be able to download their order automatically once they complete payment.

How it works

1. Buyers visit your site and place orders by clicking the Buy Now buttons that you place by the items you sell.
2. Buyers sign in to Google Checkout to confirm payment and delivery details.
3. You process the orders through the Google Checkout Merchant Centre.

To integrate using Buy Now buttons

Sign up for Google Checkout, and then click 'Buy Now buttons' under the 'Tools' tab. Place the Google-generated HTML on your website.

For more information, including step-by-step instructions, see the Developer Guide.

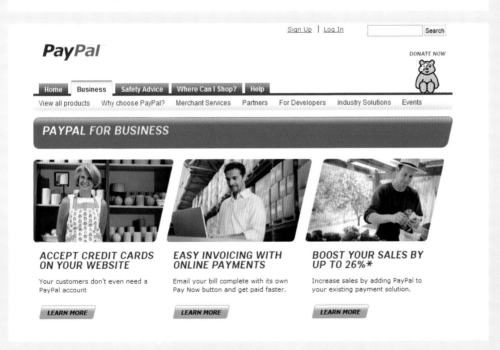

Google Checkout threatens to give PayPal a run for its money.

PayPal is the market leader for online purchasing services.

Tracking orders

Order tracking at City Link
(www.city-link.co.uk).

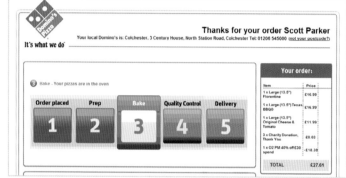

Some products might take days to arrive, but others you'll expect in minutes. Domino's Pizza offer an excellent online service that lets you track your pizza from the moment you make your order, through the cooking process, and until it is delivered to your door.

The ability to track online orders for goods has been a fantastic development in the world of ecommerce that when integrated correctly can save a lot of frustration for customers and admin work for site owners.

Some online purchases, such as services or licenses, are instant and don't require tracking. Some purchases are routine and not urgent, such as regular orders for stationery or blank media. But others are far from unimportant and can have customers waiting at their doors each day for the courier and on the phone to you when the delivery doesn't make a prompt appearance. In this last category you can put any purchases over $100, any new releases of any products of any value, gadgets, or time-sensitive shipments such as Christmas presents, Valentine's Day flowers, or perishable goods.

Quality order tracking can really improve the online shopping process, and it might even save you time and money. If anxious customers can enter their order number into your site and discover for certain that their package was dispatched that day or was delayed but will arrive before next Thursday, their minds will be put at rest and they probably won't bother you with customer service queries.

Most shopping cart packages will include an order-tracking feature, allowing customers to review their orders and check the delivery status. Many will also support the integration of the tracking services offered by third-party fulfillment companies like UPS, which can offer real-time updates of exactly where your package is.

If you don't have to deal with too many orders and can manage all the fulfillment yourself, you could take a more personal approach by simply contacting your customers to tell them when you have put it in the post.

Remember to give comprehensive confirmation of all orders on transaction screens and via email, explain clearly your stock status and estimated delivery times, and don't hesitate to report any and all delays to your customers and admit when any glitches are your fault.

Protecting customer privacy

Although ecommerce has now become an essential part of life for a large proportion of the online population, there are many people who still carry niggling doubts about their privacy and security when shopping or using premium services online. Your bottom line depends on visitors feeling totally reassured about your privacy policies and the robustness of your business. If you don't make them feel warm and safe, they'll spend their money elsewhere, and if you get a reputation for poor privacy, your venture will be dead in the water.

Your potential customers will likely be very familiar by now with making transactions online and won't flinch at spending money on a professional-looking site. But they will also have read a great deal about online fraud, identity theft, phishing scams, and other nasties that they'll be keen to avoid. An absolute must for any transactional site is to ensure that the comforting little padlock and "https" URL prefix pops up in your site's address bar when it's time for customers to make payments. You'll need an SSL (secure socket layer) certificate, the de facto standard for protecting and encrypting sensitive data sent across the public internet (like personal data or financial information). Many businesses buy these from VeriSign (www.verisign.com), now part of Symantec, but they are also available from other SSL authorities, such as GeoTrust, Thawte, or InstantSSL.

The best way to protect customer credit card data is to never store it yourself but instead use a trusted payment gateway with online reference markers placed in your own system. Card strip data like CVC numbers are particularly sensitive with modern web users, so a transactional partner is the most logical route to take. More routine customer data like identities and addresses are also sensitive, of course, but ensuring SSL is present on any

page on which you request such information is generally deemed sufficient.

If you are collecting any customer details then you should provide a privacy policy that is easily accessible on your site, commonly through a link in the footer. This will clearly outline what information you are gathering, what you will do with it, and how you will keep it secure. It is worth reading the relevant data protection legislation to check that you are doing everything that is required by law, and sample privacy policy templates are easily available for you to modify according to your needs.

Ultimately, you will gain the trust of customers as well as a reputation for being a sound online business by establishing credibility through years of transactional activity without any issues. In the meantime, people will be more willing to deal with you if you can reassure them that you're protecting their privacy in every way you can.

You can download a sample privacy policy from www.businesslink.gov.uk.

SSL is the standard protection for sensitive data.

If you want to show customers you care about their privacy, you can seek certification from companies like TRUSTe. It doesn't come free, of course, but they'll provide a custom privacy policy, a dispute resolution service, and a reassuring logo to paste onto your pages: www.truste.com.

Apple has a good reputation for their customer service. They have extensive online support and you can make a reservation for an appointment at one of their in-store Genuis Bars if you want advice in person rather than over the phone or via email.

Apple Retail Store. Come to shop. Return to learn.

Got a technical question? Step up to the Genius Bar.

When you have questions or need hands-on technical support for your Mac, iPad, iPod, Apple TV, or iPhone, you can get friendly, expert advice at the Genius Bar in any Apple Retail Store.

The Genius Bar is home to our resident Geniuses. Trained at Apple headquarters, they have extensive knowledge of Apple products and can answer all your technical questions. In fact, Geniuses can take care of everything from troubleshooting problems to actual repairs. Want to speak to a Genius? Make an appointment ahead of time to guarantee your space.

Genius Bar Reservations
To make an appointment at the Genius Bar, please select your state.

Select a State

Select a Store

Reserve

Providing great customer service

In the early days of ecommerce and web services, a company's online presence was often supplemental to its brick-and-mortar existence. It acted as just another channel to customers, alongside face-to-face transactions, telephone services, and mail ordering. The online market was still establishing itself, and so it was often deemed sufficient to provide a front-end shop window only in order to grab a pioneering advantage over competitors.

Now online commercial channels are often the main outlet for businesses, and robust and functional back-end services are nearly as important as that inviting shop window.

In crowded markets in which it is often hard to distinguish businesses in terms of products, services, or pricing alone, it is often fulfillment, support, and professionalism that will encourage customer loyalty and reduce churn. Brands such as Apple and Amazon, for example, have built enviable reputations and loyal customer bases not only for their products but for the efforts they are seen to put into their customer service.

When possible, it is always a good idea to make your support services feel open, personal, friendly, and genuinely helpful, rather than perfunctory and functional. Many customers will check that there is a direct line of communication to you should they need it before they make any transactions. But there are also steps you should consider to help customers help themselves before contacting you. An FAQ page or searchable knowledgebase can often filter out low-level queries quickly and simply, as can help captions embedded into forms. If you need to offer technical support too, you can provide tutorials or manuals.

You can provide more direct customer service in several ways or in any combination, but you must make the decision yourself over which methods will work best in your market and what level of service you are able to maintain consistently. Do not offer a level of customer service that you are unable to fulfill.

The primary channel of direct support, particularly for companies with business premises, remains the telephone. Customers are just much happier spending money with a website that puts its contact telephone number on every page and promotes free or low-cost helplines, even if they don't actually use them. Live online support is an option if you have the resources, although some users might shy away from you if you invite them for a chat without them asking for it.

Email support is preferable to many consumers who would rather not speak to you directly, but it is important to immediately acknowledge receipt of emails and give a firm commitment as to when you will respond in full—and to keep those promises. Customers will put up with a surprising amount of disruption or delay as long as they are courteously and honestly kept fully informed about progress. Problems will inevitably occur from time to time, but nothing impresses a customer more than when you exceed their expectations in your efforts to rectify the issue.

Whatever help you provide or communications you send to your customer, the language you use should be clear, easy to understand, and free from jargon if possible, but you also need to show you know what you are talking about. Keep the tone friendly and reassuring—an informal and personal approach is often more appreciated than a straight technical answer, as it makes people feel like they are dealing with humans and not just a computer.

User surveys and reviews

Online consumers are far more discerning than you might imagine. Certainly it's possible to lure them with a skillful viral marketing campaign here or a sustained body of brand buzz work there. But loyal customers will only be retained if they are genuinely impressed by your products, services, and fulfillment.

That is why word-of-mouth recommendations and peer reviews are so highly valued by online consumers and online businesses alike. Consumers trust the opinions of people like themselves, who have a choice where they spend their time and money, more than they believe the claims of vendors and service providers with a vested interest in saying their wares are the best. If you're good at what you do, your customers will evangelize your business. But they'll tell more people about the great job you're doing if you make it as easy as possible for them to do so.

It's important to know what your customers or users really think about your business. There are a variety of methods you can employ to find out the truth, but online questionnaires and surveys are a useful starting point.

Low-cost tools such as the ever-popular SurveyMonkey (www.surveymonkey.com) are cheap and rapid to initiate and are a familiar and acceptable part of the online consumer experience. Surveys can be easily ignored by busy visitors but will usually provide you with a broad impression of your business that will help you shape services in the future far better than isolated knee-jerk opinions. Just remember to keep the question list brief, tight, and optional. Incentives, such as discount vouchers, can also speed up the process of gaining a suitable volume of responses.

If your business is relatively mature with a high volume of regular customers, community features such as forums can provide you with an ever-present (if somewhat partial) customer focus group to dip into for ideas and reactions.

Perhaps the most common way for a modern start-up online commercial business to get feedback is to put in the hours with social media then simply ask for feedback through Facebook, Twitter, and any other platforms that appeal to customers. Of course you'll need total confidence in your business or a thick skin to filter all the comments, but it's still a very useful and immediate route to consider.

All of which leads to one warning about seeking the views of your customers. As with most areas of website design, development, and management, there are pros and cons to user feedback. On the plus side, if you are able to think objectively and impartially about your business, then feedback can provide you with invaluable insights into what your customers really think about you and the service you provide. Feedback can directly identify easily (and not so easily) fixable design issues or functionality glitches on your site that can be tweaked to improve customer experiences. Sometimes a well-meaning critical eye can pinpoint issues that you'd otherwise never have considered.

But the flipside to this usefulness is the less well-meaning feedback that will inevitably follow any request for opinions. If you seek a range of opinions, you will get them, and some of them might upset you. So stay level-headed, react evenly to all comments positive and negative, don't initiate radical

SurveyMonkey is a good resource for garnering customer feedback on your website: www.surveymonkey.com.

actions in response to minority opinions without really thinking things through, don't take overly critical feedback to heart if at all possible, and remember that just like the process of building your business itself, understanding your customers and users is also a learning curve that takes time to master.

Some online stores give their customers the opportunity to rate the products they have purchased. There is no doubt that dozens of five-star reviews will be a strong incentive for others to buy, but what happens if something you are desperately trying to shift doesn't fare so well? Some sites might be tempted to conveniently forget showing the less favorable reviews, but that could just make matters worse if someone notices and sounds off elsewhere.

Dabs.com displays customer reviews and product ratings.

Clear pricing, terms, and shipping

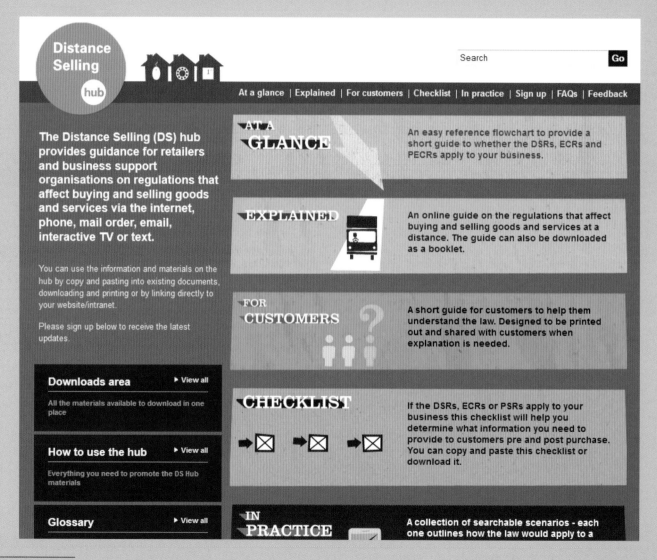

Distance Selling hub

Search [_____] [Go]

At a glance | Explained | For customers | Checklist | In practice | Sign up | FAQs | Feedback

The Distance Selling (DS) hub provides guidance for retailers and business support organisations on regulations that affect buying and selling goods and services via the internet, phone, mail order, email, interactive TV or text.

You can use the information and materials on the hub by copy and pasting into existing documents, downloading and printing or by linking directly to your website/intranet.

Please sign up below to receive the latest updates.

Downloads area ▶ View all
All the materials available to download in one place

How to use the hub ▶ View all
Everything you need to promote the DS Hub materials

Glossary ▶ View all

AT A GLANCE
An easy reference flowchart to provide a short guide to whether the DSRs, ECRs and PECRs apply to your business.

EXPLAINED
An online guide on the regulations that affect buying and selling goods and services at a distance. The guide can also be downloaded as a booklet.

FOR CUSTOMERS
A short guide for customers to help them understand the law. Designed to be printed out and shared with customers when explanation is needed.

CHECKLIST
If the DSRs, ECRs or PSRs apply to your business this checklist will help you determine what information you need to provide to customers pre and post purchase. You can copy and paste this checklist or download it.

IN PRACTICE
A collection of searchable scenarios - each one outlines how the law would apply to a

One final consideration for the transactional side of your web business is to make sure you are as clear and transparent as possible about the services you are actually offering and the money you are charging for your services.

It sounds like obvious advice, but you would be surprised by how many online businesses fall at this last hurdle by not making the total cost of services clear until the shopping cart has been totaled. Nothing will send your potential customers running into the arms of a rival website quite like confusing pricing structures and perceived hidden costs. They need to know what value they are getting for their money.

Some businesses obviously offer far more complex services and more varied pricing options than others, so it is up to you to make a checklist of all variables and then make those evident to site visitors. Show pricing boldly, make it clear whether sales taxes are included, and state from the very start of each transaction whether there are any additional charges for using credit cards or online payment services.

Also, consider spending some time creating service policies that your customers can understand and that you are able to honor. If your ordering process might be considered complex for first-time visitors, think about writing a guide. If order cancelations will cost your business, then let customers know the price of changing or canceling their orders, or indeed if there is no charge for the service. Agree your actions in the event of lost orders, lost shipments, or stock delays. Write all these terms and conditions very clearly in plain English and flag them as obvious and available for all customers to consult on every transactional page.

Also, don't forget to detail your shipping promises. If you have a lot of competitors selling similar products or services, delivery becomes a very important issue in the minds of customers. Drive down shipping costs as low as you can so that you can proudly display those costs (or even an offer of free shipping on bulk orders). Let customers know the service that will be fulfilling their orders (digital delivery, postal service, or other courier) and where applicable, flag up third-party tracking tools, as described elsewhere in this chapter.

Being upfront with your customers isn't just good practice, it is the law. To make sure you don't get in any legal hot water, it is worth checking the relevant legislation for online businesses.

The Office of Fair Trading's Distance Selling Hub offers comprehensive guidance on the various regulations: www.oft.gov.uk

Chapter 9
Accessibility

Why accessibility is important

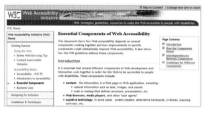

Web pages can be rated according to how well they conform to the W3C web content accessibility guideline. If you manage the tricky task of following all the priority checkpoints, you can add the AAA logo to your website.

Wave is a free accessibility evaluation tool—just put in your website address to see if it is up to scratch: wave.webaim.org.

Each of us creates and maintains business and personal websites for a broad range of reasons. They extend our brand, identity, awareness, and market position by establishing a structured presence on the internet. They enable us to open up new channels of communication, information, sales, services, and community.

Above all, they provide us with a location where we can interact with our stakeholders, partners, customers, colleagues, friends, and family.

To maximize the value and effectiveness of all of this creative effort to engage with the online population, it makes good sense to make our sites as welcoming as possible for as many people as possible. Web accessibility is important because it is concerned with making websites inclusive and usable for visitors of all abilities. Accessibility guidelines are constantly tailored to ensure that carefully designed and developed websites provide an equal level of access to all, delivering information and services to as wide a possible audience as desired.

The World Wide Web Consortium (W3C) is at the forefront of the movement to ensure web accessibility awareness and adoption remains a high priority for developers. Its stated mission will strike a chord with any site owner: to lead the web to its full potential. Web inventor and W3C director Tim Berners-Lee believes, "The power of the Web is in its universality. Access by everyone regardless of disability is an essential aspect." Because the web was designed from the very beginning to support everybody regardless of their hardware, software, physical, or mental ability, accessibility is fundamental to its success.

Any designer or developer must understand the web's role in removing the type of exclusions and barriers of access that still litter physical society. The UN Convention on the Rights of Persons with Disabilities (www.un.org/disabilities/convention/conventionfull.shtml) now states that access to information and communications technologies is a basic human right, but there are also practical benefits of accessibility for any business.

Accessible sites achieve better search results. They embrace a larger audience of visitors or potential customers, their ordered designs pave the way for easy migration to other channels (such as mobile), they promote social inclusion that is core to online communities, and they generally cost less to maintain because they are built intelligently in the first instance.

Fortunately, there's plenty of guidance available to help us make our websites accessible. The W3C's Web Accessibility Initiative or WAI (www.w3.org/WAI) combines the varied talents of individuals from the technology industry, disability organizations, government bodies, and research labs to provide accessibility guidelines and tools to make our sites, social media platforms, and web applications usable and inviting for people with any disabilities.

Understanding
assistive devices

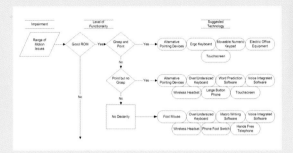

Microsoft's Assistive Technology Design Tree: www.microsoft.com/enable/business/identifytech.aspx.

The Guild of Accessible Web Designers provides an excellent summary of the assistive devices available (www.gawds.org).

Assistive Technology: Braille and Low Vision Aids

Braille Displays

Replaces the computer monitor and is often augmented with Speech Output Systems. A line of Braille cells gives a tactile representation of the computer's text output.

Assistive devices, together with assistive technology, are gadgets and processes that assist disabled people to perform tasks online more easily than they would otherwise be able to do with standard computer equipment.

The goal of assistive technology is universal accessibility through intelligent design. For many people, a QWERTY keyboard, mouse, and standard display don't represent practical computing equipment. Perhaps their motor skills are impaired, or their sight, hearing, or posture. Fortunately, an expanding range of innovative devices is coming to the market all the time, delivering greater independence and a far more enjoyable online experience for a significant proportion of internet users.

After decades of research, there are of course some commonplace areas of assistive device development, notably alternative input devices, alternative output devices, visual alerts for the hearing impaired, audio alerts for the visually impaired, reading tools, speech synthesizers, speech recognition software, ergonomics, and a variety of alternative screen technologies.

Many of us grumble at the aches and pains we get from cramped keyboards and cranky mice—niggles we could easily overcome by addressing our postures and investing in assistive ergonomic keyboards or pointing devices that better suit our working habits. But what are the options for people with serious impairments?

Well, they start very logically: large tracker balls, scroll wheels, wands, sticks, or foot-operated mice, coupled with keyboards featuring large numerals, high contrast keys, locator dots, "chorded" keys that enable combinations of presses of just a few keys to produce all letters, or even direct voice control and speech recognition software.

But far smarter input devices are also now available, such as cursors controlled by eye tracking or brain activity; flexible touchscreens that can be tailored to the sensitivity and habits of individual users; and even sip-and-puff devices that allow people with a high degree of physical disability to control interfaces with their breathing.

Each area of impairment now has a similarly impressive array of assistive technology development working to bring universal accessibility closer. Microsoft even has a product called the Assistive Technology Design Tree specifically to help users identify the right assistive technology products for them (www.microsoft.com/enable/business/identifytech.aspx).

The majority of assistive devices are now built tightly to industry standards and W3C/WAI guidelines, so it is vital that you follow their lead to ensure your websites and web applications truly are fully accessible. Otherwise you'll never reach anybody who wants to use your services and buy your products using technology like refreshable Braille displays or customized speech synthesizers. Such devices are opening up new online experiences for their users, but they are also opening up new audiences for online businesses.

Providing alternative content

See colourblindawareness.org for examples of how color-blind people see the world, or use the helpful accessibility tools at www.etre.com.

The ultimate goal of web accessibility is for all businesses and individuals to work to ensure that their main website is as accessible as possible, rather than choosing to make accessible "versions" of the site for some of their visitors.

Instead of ripping out core graphics, colors, style sheets, navigation, multimedia, and so on to create a stripped-down textual site that may be technically more accessible, everybody would much rather see the richer elements remain, but be used more intelligently. Text-only sites are of little advantage to users with mobility or cognitive impairments, who also would like the full graphical experience wherever possible.

Of course, this isn't to say that there aren't accessibility considerations for the use of colors and graphics. We have already covered the fact that people with impaired vision have issues not only with font sizes but also with color contrast between the foreground and background of text panels. Don't forget the eight percent of men and one percent of women who are affected by color blindness—red doesn't mean danger for people who cannot distinguish it from green. Color coding can still be used to help the learning-disabled if used logically, predictably, and with care, but try not to use color alone. Similarly, graphics and photos can be a major advantage to accessibility with just a few additional considerations.

Leonard Cheshire Disability has created adverts to highlight the issues faced by disabled people, all with the option of subtitles or sign language instead of audio: www.creaturediscomforts.org.

It's not only written web content that should be informative and functional. Each visual element on a website should always be useful and add something to the general understanding of the site's function. Irrelevant images can confuse some visitors and will certainly hinder the operation of many assistive devices. If the images are well thought out, then alternative text can be added to each of them to inform screen readers.

A potentially indistinct image of a building, enhanced with alt text that prompts a screen reader to identify the building, would clearly be of great benefit to the visually impaired. Similarly useful alternative text can be added to maps, signs, symbols, buttons, movie clips—any non-textual visual element that can be made more practical. Sometimes, of course, alternatives must be a little more inventive. A graph or chart should be described so its meaning can be more easily translated, for example into speech or Braille. This is particularly useful when

visually impaired people are watching presentations. Conversely, any audio files can be transcribed into annotated text documents, and videos may be subtitled and described.

At its most effective, alternative content must actually be "equivalent" to original content, performing the exact same role and being functional in different ways for different visitors.

Ensuring accessible navigation

W3C° **Web Accessibility initiative**

WAI: Strategies, guidelines, resources to make the Web accessible to people with disabilities

W3C Home

Web Accessibility Initiative (WAI) Home

Getting Started

Using the Web

>> • **Better Web Browsing Tips**

• Contact Inaccessible Websites

Accessibility Basics

• Accessibility - W3C ⬉

• Introduction to Accessibility

• Essential Components

• Business Case

Designing for Inclusion

Better Web Browsing: Tips for Customizing Your Computer
[Draft updated 24 May 2010]

This document provides references to resources, including detailed documentation and step-by-step guides, to help you customize your particular web browser and computer setup.

Page Contents

▼ Introduction
▼ Optimize Your Computer Setup
▼ **Difficulty Seeing and Reading Websites?**
    ▼ Enlarging Text and Images
    ▼ Changing Colors and Fonts
    ▼ Listening Rather than Reading
▼ **Difficulty Hearing Audio on Websites?**
    ▼ Adjusting the Volume
    ▼ Captions and Transcripts
    ▼ Sign Language Videos

Excellent W3C recommendation guidelines are in place to help developers in their efforts to make it easier for all people to find what they are looking for online, especially those with visual or cognitive impairments.

Clear, simple content demands intuitive website navigation that enables all visitors to move within and between pages using mechanisms they can quickly understand. Developers can use a range of navigation tools and additional information to make their sites as accessible, and friendly, as possible for users who find standard navigation tricky.

Standard web navigation relies upon visitors being able to view the entire content of pages and to use visual cues to grasp in moments how they are supposed to access the information they are looking for. Sight impairments can render basic visual clues useless, while visitors who can only view part of each page at a time through the use of screen readers or magnified or Braille displays can find sites bewildering when navigation mechanisms become disjointed and out of context. Even the addition of some basic structural metadata can help visitors determine where they are within a site and perform some initial page-to-page navigation thanks to basic author, content, and keyword information.

Too often lazy design leaves visitors who are visually impaired listening to their screen readers reeling off seemingly endless lists of menu buttons mixed with secondary content links, advertising, and other confusing messages. Sighted visitors who are unable to use a mouse or other traditional pointing devices can be similarly frustrated by having to tab through pages repeatedly in order to reach the content they came for.

One way to ensure accessible navigation is to provide a well-directed "skip to main content" option at the very start of each page. This lets visitors jump past repetitive, templated, horizontal, and vertical navigation bars straight to the core information. Each of these links can serve as an accessibility "anchor" as long as it is obvious to its intended audience and includes

alternative text. It can be hidden in headers if desired, but it's more common these days to make accessibility information obvious to all.

In-page navigation can also be improved dramatically with a list of "jump links" that can be more efficiently tabbed or read through by visitors looking for a shortcut to a particular content section of interest. As you might expect, the W3C website does this superbly, prefixing every lengthy page with a contents table of links that jump down to the relevant information, and is a great example of the approach. The most popular modern screen readers also use a technique called "headings navigation" to make pages that haven't been organized like this work in a similar way, as long as headings are clear and obvious.

Many web applications increasingly use technologies like JavaScript and Ajax to create complex user-interface controls. While features like tree navigation, drag-and-drop, and sliders can really improve the user experience for many people, those using screen readers or unable to use a mouse might be left struggling. WAI-ARIA—the Accessible Rich Applications Suite—provides a framework to help make dynamic web content more accessible by adding roles, states, and properties to elements to help people with disabilities navigate your pages. A standard has yet to be agreed, but it is widely supported by browsers and assistive technologies and so should be investigated if you are serious about accessibility. Find out more at www.w3.org/WAI/intro/aria.php.

Consistency in navigation is arguably the greatest aid for accessibility. With adaptive technology in place, most visitors can quickly get a feel for where they are on a page and where the content they need is likely to be, as long as each page is arranged logically and in the same way.

Enabling keyboard control

Microsoft's much-loved StickyKeys, introduced for Windows 95 but still going strong, is a great example of a mainstream keyboard accessibility tool.

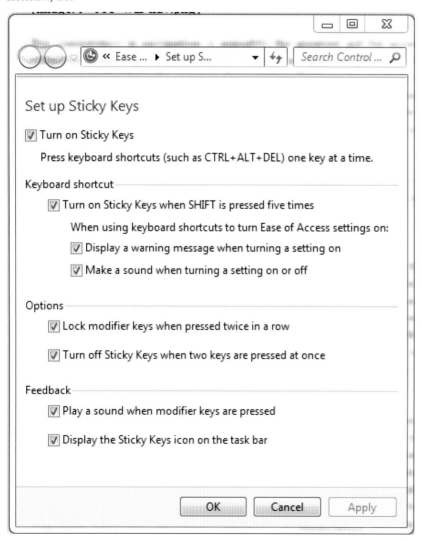

You might think that keyboards are complicated, clunky, and far from user-friendly for anyone with accessibility issues. But actually they perform a major role in aiding web navigation for the many thousands of computer users who have impaired vision or motor skills and find mice and tracker balls pretty useless. Even people who cannot physically use keyboards rely heavily on predictable keyboard controls as the bedrock for their own access, so it is vital that all websites are keyboard accessible in order to ensure that a larger audience than you might think doesn't find itself excluded.

Fortunately all mainstream modern web browsers now include provision for a keyboard user interface, or UI. A keyboard UI allows any site to be navigated with a keyboard alone, using either single keystrokes or combination shortcuts depending on preference. Some vendors, particularly those challenged with developing natural keyboard navigation for web applications, have come up with replacement systems that replace multiple key inputs—such as CTRL/ALT/DELETE—with sequential shortcuts.

A good keyboard UI also serves as the foundation for a lot of assistive technology, including screen readers, screen enlargers, puff-and-sip, voice inputs, single switches, and other devices. All of these methods ultimately mimic keyboard inputs at some stage. So for the richest experience for all, keyboard navigation should strive to be equivalent to mouse navigation in every instance. It should also be flexible, enabling users to customize functions and shortcut methods to better suit their own habits and needs. Once configured though, keyboard commands should be rigidly consistent and should never be switched unexpectedly, causing a frustrating user experience.

Access key scheme

Access keys let you navigate around a website without using a mouse. You may find them a convenient way to move round the site without having to move your mouse at all.

Access keys on Directgov

Directgov uses the following access keys:

s - Skip navigation
1 - Home page
2 - Newsroom
3 - Site index
4 - Search
6 - Help
7 - Complaints
8 - Terms and conditions
0 - Access key details

Skip navigation on any given page allows you to bypass the navigation areas and go directly to that page's main content.

Directgov outlines the access keys for their website in the Accessibility pages: www.direct.gov.uk

Although enabling keyboard control is as important as ever, modern site editing platforms have evolved admirably to embrace the concept. Homepage keys, main content skips, header tabbing, and finer cursor control are all recommended as fundamental tools. Content management systems are also not bad at adding accessibility features out of the box, but exactly what keyboard control is available will depend on the theme you are using.

You can set "access keys" in your HTML to allow keyboard command to take you to a particular page. For example, if you add <a href="/search" accesskey="4">, pressing Alt+4 would take you to the search page.

The problem with setting access keys is that there is currently no agreed international standard for which shortcuts should be used for what. It's also the case that any access keys you add could conflict with those in the browser or with assistive technology, so it's worth checking what combinations are the safest options.

Whatever keyboard control you add, it is worth explaining it on a separate "accessibility options" page that can be easily found by those that might need it.

You should also check that elements such as tab orders, shortcuts, and skip navigation perform as expected and are optimized through real-world testing.

For further reading, Web Accessibility in Mind lists some excellent practical considerations for all site owners to bear in mind: (webaim.org/techniques/keyboard).

Flash accessibility

J.K. Rowling
official site

▷ accessibility tools

Car driving past

1965 - 2011

29 / 09 / 11
Wizard of the
Month Archive

BIGGEST EVER ISSUE!
ALL NEW LATEST
RUMOURS!

The Daily News

The Daily News | Est March, 03, 2004   www.jkrowling.com

POTTERMORE

You may have recently noticed a number of owls on various websites leading you to a YouTube film, where I have announced my latest, exciting piece of n...

POTTERMORE is a new web site, where you can enjoy an online experience based around the Harry Potter books, which includes exclusive new information from me. If you...

Everything you might want to know

J K (Joanne Kathleen) Rowling was born in July 1965 at Yate General Hospital in England and grew up in Chepstow, Gwent where she went to Wyedean Comprehensive.

Jo left Chepstow for Exeter University, where she...

Site by Lightmaker

J.K. Rowling's official website is built entirely with Flash but still keeps accessibility in mind: www.jkrowling.com.

When Flash was born, it was lauded as a way for web designers to add exciting video and animation to websites and make the internet more fun, but it soon became the bane of accessibility champions everywhere. Flash has never quite become a ubiquitous technology embraced by all browsers and devices, and, as a result, it has often been criticized for disrupting the usability and accessibility of websites. Despite this, Flash is still popular and widely used and, with a little effort, most of its perceived accessibility issues can now be resolved.

Nobody takes Flash accessibility more seriously these days than Adobe itself. Although there are many sources of advice available for Flash developers with accessibility at the front of their minds, there is actually no substitute for the vendor's own advice. Flash has come a long way, and while there are still issues, it is now more accessible with every revision.

The latest versions, Adobe's Flash CS and Flash Player, have been developed to include users of assistive technology, but web designers still need to use the software intelligently to ensure an accessible and rich user experience, even in conjunction with screen readers and other devices. It's definitely worth adhering to the important guidelines if you are thinking of using Flash, as endorsed by the Adobe user community: www.adobe.com/accessibility/products/flash/best_practices.html.

As with any accessible website design, color schemes and contrasts must be taken into account, and it remains essential to provide text equivalents for all graphical elements and group them logically. This includes buttons, icons, and animations. Films and animations should not be looped if possible, as they can drive screen readers crazy, and extra consideration should be paid to making the content of these elements smooth with as few rapid changes as possible. Clear movie navigation buttons are also always welcome, as is as much control as possible over when audio or video is permitted at all.

Flash actually includes a broad range of accessibility components for developers that can automate best practices such as keyboard navigation and accessibility pre-tests to fine-tune inclusive design. Developers can access accessibility aids at any point during design by using the command "enableAccessibility()." You should ensure operations such as keyboard control of movies are intuitive and that alternative text for the sight impaired and closed captions for those with hearing difficulties are all as useful as they can be. When multimedia elements get really complex, such as blockbuster movie clips, it's also an excellent idea to provide descriptive narration in audio and text to explain the action in real-time.

Nobody pretends that Flash content is as easy to make accessible as basic textual information, but a richer experience can be a far more direct and practical way for many disabled web users to get the information they need fast. Accessibility guidelines from Adobe, W3C, and Section 508 (www.section508.gov) all contribute to efficient and considerate use of Flash, but practical validation is always the best test before real-world deployment. If possible, Flash sites should be road-tested using assistive technology and keyboard access in a variety of combinations, while nothing beats the feedback of real people interested in making rich, interactive content work for them, rather than settling for having it all stripped out.

Chapter 10
Going Live

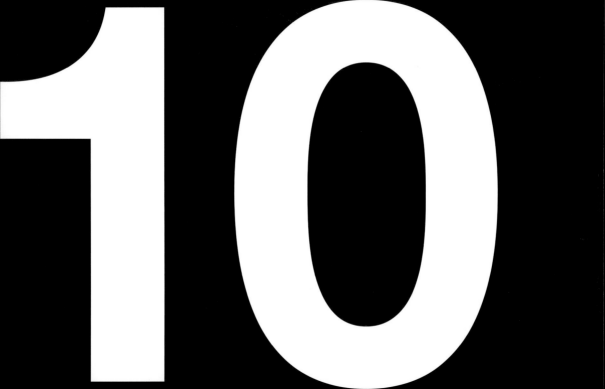

Testing

Bug-tracking packages like www.bugzilla.org help you manage your website's software development.

Testing is often forgotten in all the excitement of finishing your website, but you'll want to make sure that everyone sees your wonderful creation as you'd like them to. You should have tested your pages as you've gone along, but it is worth taking some time at the end to double-check that everything is working properly.

You can easily view HTML files on your computer through your web browser, but if you are using a dynamic scripting language like PHP you'll need a web server to test your pages. You could push your files up to your web space with your FTP software and set up a test domain for your site, but it is also useful to set up a local web server on your computer. How you do this will depend on the language you are using and what server environment you have, but check out EasyPHP (www.easy-php.org) or see learn.iis.net if you need to use Microsoft IIS.

The first thing you'll need to do is check your pages on all web browsers. You should have the latest versions of all the main browsers installed, but it is likely to be the older ones that could cause you problems. You can use premium services like Adobe Browser Labs (browserlab.adobe.com)—which is integrated into Dreamweaver—or BrowserCam (www.browsercam.com), but if Internet Explorer

is your main concern you could try IETester at www.my-debugbar.com/wiki/IETester/HomePage.

You'll need to cater for people using both huge monitors and small screens, so don't forget to take a look at your site at different resolutions. Check out resizemybrowser.com or use the Firefox Web Developer Toolbar. Whether or not you have created separate style sheets for mobile and print, you should also check to see how your pages look on paper and on a range of mobile devices.

Although you might be able whizz through the site to make sure everything is working, the real test is to put it in front of some proper users. They might be able to spot things you have missed or not know how to do things that seem obvious to you.

However you brief your testers, they will inevitably stray away from finding bugs and will suggest changes to design and functionality. If you've done your research properly and have spoken to existing or potential users before building your new website, then they should not flag up any major issues, but take heed of everything they say and take action if they are all saying the same thing.

If there are several people developing and testing your site, you should have some kind of issue log to keep track of what needs fixing and by whom. A simple shared Google Docs spreadsheet might be all you need, but there are many bug-tracking packages available like JIRA (www.atlassian.com/jira) and Bugzilla (www.bugzilla.org).

If you are expecting thousands of people to come flooding to your site, you'll want to make sure your site can cope with the pressure. All might run smoothly when there's just a few people downloading videos or accessing a database, but what will happen when there are a hundred people doing it at the same time? If you're dealing with complex business-critical applications, you'll want professional load-testing software such as that provided at www.webperformance.com or www.loadtestingtool.com, but for many the online service at loadimpact.com will be sufficient.

If you are using a dynamic
scripting language like PHP
you'll need a web server to
test your pages such as:
www.easyphp.org.

resizeMyBrowser

320 x 480 iPhone 3G/3GS	**480 x 320** iPhone 3G/3GS	**1024 x 600** Most Netbooks	+ create a new preset
480 x 720 Meizu M8	**720 x 480** Meizu M8	**1280 x 800** MacBook Air 08	
480 x 800 Google Nexus one	**800 x 480** Google Nexus one	**1366 x 768** Some Laptops	
640 x 960 iPhone 4	**960 x 640** iPhone 4	**1440 x 900** MacBook Pro 15 inches	
768 x 1024 iPad	**1024 x 768** iPad	**Maximum** Resize to Maximum	

Current Inner   **1280 x 939**

Outer means outerWindow size (including toolbar, addressbar and such).
Inner means innerWindow size (interior of the browser window).

Inner ▭ Outer

Ensure your site looks as
intended at different resolutions
and screen sizes, for example
at: resizemybrowser.com.

You should make sure your
website can handle the number
of visitors you are expecting by
load-testing with services like:
loadimpact.com.

Launching your site

Domain Data

Domain name : curiositytree.co.uk

DNS Settings : DNS Check

General settings : ● DNS ○ CNAME

Basic DNS Settings

Name server : [My name server ▼]

Advanced DNS Settings

Primary name server : [a1.nameserver.net]

Secondary name server : [My secondary name server ▼] (?)

1. Secondary name server [a2.nameserver.net]

2. Secondary name server [ ]

3. Secondary name server [ ]

Make sure you change the name server to direct people to the right place if your domain name is registered with a different provider to the one that hosts your web server.

You've finished all the testing, everything is looking perfect, and at last the time has come to launch your website. You have come too far to fall at the final hurdle, so don't rush into it—you need a clear plan of action, and you'll want to take every precaution to make sure it all goes smoothly.

Before you push the button to make your new site live, ensure that you have a backup of the old pages just in case. If things don't go quite to plan when you launch your new site, you can always restore the old one. It also means you'll have a record of old content just in case you have forgotten to copy anything across to your new pages.

Launching a website will involve transferring files to your web server, but you might also need to amend the Domain Name System (DNS) settings. How you do this will depend on where you have registered your domain, but most registrars will give you a simple control panel to make the necessary changes. If you already have your site up and running on your web server on a test URL, then going live might simply be a case of changing the destination directory for the main domain. If your domain name is registered with a different provider to the one that hosts your web server, you will need to change the "name servers" for the domain to point to the correct place.

Note that DNS updates won't happen instantaneously and that the changes might work for some of your visitors before others as they are propagated around the world. This is usually within a few hours for most people but can take a couple of days—so don't go making any big announcements until you are sure everyone will be seeing your new site properly.

```
1   ErrorDocument 404 /404.html
2
3   RewriteEngine On
4   rewritecond %{http_host} ^scottparker.co.uk
5   rewriteRule ^(.*) http://www.scottparker.co.uk/$1 [R=301,L]
6
7   Redirect 301 /index.html http://www.www.scottparker.co.uk/index.php
8   Redirect 301 /about.html http://www.scottparker.co.uk/about-us.php
9   Redirect 301 /product.html http://www.www.scottparker.co.uk/services.php
10  Redirect 301 /contact.html http://www.scottparker.co.uk/contact-us.php
11
```

301 redirects with Linux can be
implemented with a .htaccess
configuration file, but you can
find plenty of further information
on Google to help you.

With this in mind, you should choose a good time for when you want the site to go live. This isn't so important if you are building something completely new, but if you are replacing an existing website then you should avoid potentially busy periods just in case things go awry. A Saturday evening is often a safe bet, although you'll also need to make sure everyone involved is available to make it all go smoothly.

You might want to wait for some initial feedback to make sure everything is perfect before you tell everyone about your site. A popular tactic is to go for a "soft launch," where you quietly push the site live, maybe even on a different URL, and slowly direct people there to see what they think. This gives you time to fix any bugs or typos you might have missed and will hopefully confirm what a great job you've done. If all is ship-shape, you can simply switch the domain and then tell the world.

If you are replacing an old website and changing all the filenames, it is essential that you set up redirects from the old URLs to the new pages. You don't want people to follow an old link to your site and be faced with a "404 Page Not Found" error. Search engines might have indexed your pages too, and if their spiders find that your pages have disappeared, you might lose valuable search engine ranking. Redirects—or 301 redirects in this case—should be done on the server. With Linux this is done with the .htaccess configuration file, a simple text file placed in your website directory that gives instructions to the server. If you are changing your domain name, you can also redirect the old domain to the new one using the same file. You'll find plenty of information about how to add redirects to .htaccess with a quick search on Google. For Windows environments you'll need to access IIS on the server to set 301 redirects, although you might be able to control IIS with a web.config file.

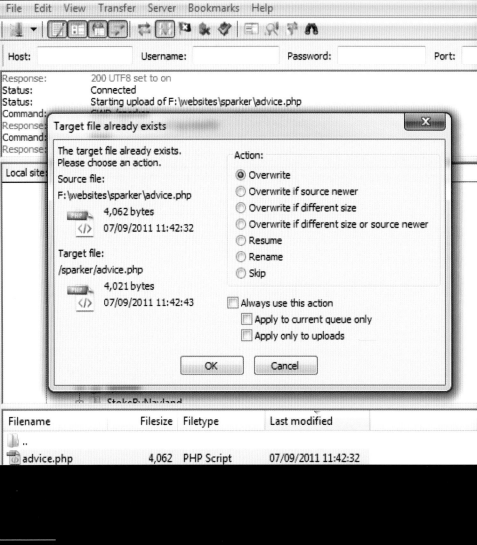

086

It's important to keep regular backups of your website, especially when overwriting old content.

Ensure that all old links to deleted content are removed. You can use the service at W3C to check your links: validator. w3.org/checklink.

One of the joys of publishing on the web is that you can add or amend content quickly and easily whenever you need to. What is often more difficult is finding the time and inclination to manage the site and make sure that everything is fresh and up to date.

There are few bigger turn-offs than a two-year-old news story adorning your homepage or links to events that have long been and gone. You need to remove out-of-date content, add all your latest news, and check that all the information on your site is still relevant.

A content management system will make all this much easier, but if you are updating the HTML manually and transferring files back and forth from the server, be sure you are replacing the correct ones. It is worth making regular backups of your site just in case you inadvertently copy over a crucial file.

If you change file names or delete content, make sure that there are no links back to the content you have removed, including any search engine listings or other links on external sites. If you can't edit the links yourself, set up 301 redirects to the new content. There are various browser add-ons and plug-ins for content management systems to help you check for broken links, or you can try the W3C's online service at validator.w3.org/checklink.

Make sure you test any pages you have amended and read through any text once more to make sure it all makes sense. If you are making any changes to the layout and styles, remember to do your cross-browser checks too.

It's important to be clear about who's responsibility it is to update the website—who writes the content? Who has the necessary

W3C® Link Checker
Check links and anchors in Web pages or full Web sites

Enter the address (URL) of a document that you would like to check:

www.scottparker.co.uk

More Options

- Summary only
- Hide redirects: ● all ○ for directories only
- Don't send the `Accept-Language` header
- Don't send the `Referer` header
- Check linked documents recursively, recursion depth:

- Save options in a cookie

access? Who agrees any changes? You'll also need to be clear about how the process works. Will new content be provided in a Word document for someone to turn into HTML? Are people able to edit all the content directly through the content management system? Will changes need to be agreed on a test site before going live?

If you are managing a website for a client or if someone else will be updating your site, make sure there is some sort of maintenance agreement in place. This should cover how many hours of support will be provided each month, what kinds of changes are covered, and how quickly any amendments are expected to be made.

Managing users

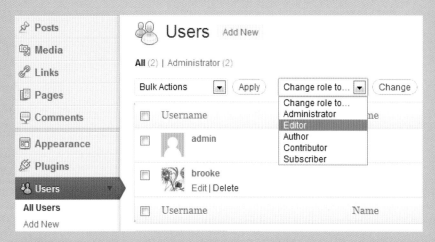

You can set different levels of access for individual users by giving them a user-type such as "editor" or "administrator," as seen here in WordPress.

If you are using WordPress, the Askimet plug-in provides comment-spam protection. Other content management systems will offer something similar.

Although it might be nice to have complete control of what goes onto your website, much of the time that just isn't possible. Sometimes you will have to rely on other people to update content, and you might also want your visitors to contribute their own posts and comments. Managing your users is an important part of maintaining your site, so make sure you are clear about who can do what.

If you are nervous about letting other people loose on your site, then you should be able to restrict their access to just what they need. Content management systems will have different user types limited to different functions, so an "editor" might be able to add and edit content for any page or post but won't be able to change any themes or plug-ins. If people are updating files by FTP, you might be able to limit their access to particular directories so they can't inadvertently copy over key files.

Make sure that anyone editing your pages has a secure password and remove users if they no longer need access—you don't want a disgruntled ex-employee logging in and wreaking havoc on your website.

If you are giving visitors to your site the opportunity to comment on your content, you'll need to decide who can say what. Is it a free-for-all, or do people have to register as a user first? Do registrations need to be approved before they can comment? You will usually be on safer ground if you restrict access to registered users, but that might mean you get less feedback.

You'll want to keep an eye on what people are saying, whoever they are, because you don't want your site to contain anything offensive or libelous, and you don't want competitors pushing their products on your pages. Check your site regularly, but most content management systems can be set

Plug-ins like the reCaptcha widget offered by Google (google.com/recaptcha) offer protection against spam-bots.

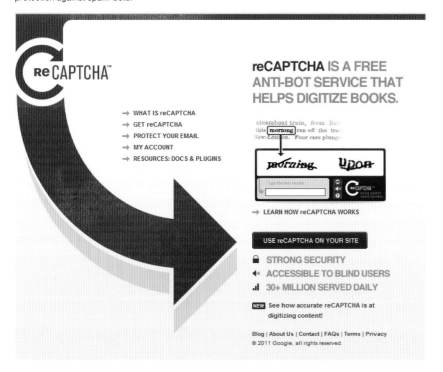

up to email you each time someone makes a comment or adds new content. If you really want to play it safe, you can insist that all content is edited and approved by you before it appears on your site, although this might not go down well with some users.

If you do have someone who is repeatedly abusing your site, you might be able to block them as a user. Of course, they might be able to just sign up as a new user under a different name. And if they are really persistent, it can be difficult to stop them without completely blocking new registrations.

Strange as it might sound, not everyone contributing to your site will be human. There are many automated robots wandering the web creating false user accounts and submitting nonsense content. It can be extremely tedious keeping on top of this junk unless you take action to prevent the machines doing their dirty work. Most content management systems will offer some kind of comment-spam protection, like the Askimet plug-in for WordPress.

You can also add a security question on forms that should only be answerable by humans—typically an image that shows some disguised letters or a simple math question.

If you have a busy community with hundreds of people contributing to your site, you'll need some help keeping on top of it all. If you give regular and trusted users the power to edit posts and to approve and remove users, you might find that your community can police itself with little intervention from you.

Monitoring traffic

The "in-page analytics" gives you valuable data on specific pages, so you can monitor things like your links on that page.

Google Analytics (www.google.com/analytics) is an excellent way to monitor your traffic. The Dashboard displays a wealth of handy statistics helping you work out the volume and quality of visits to your website.

Once everything is up and running, you'll want to know if anyone is actually visiting your site and what they are looking at.

There are many different traffic-monitoring services, but by far the most popular is Google Analytics (www.google.com/analytics). It's extremely comprehensive and easy to use, but, amazingly, it's also completely free. You simply register for the service and then add a small piece of code to every page on your site. There are plug-ins that make the process very straightforward for content management systems, or you can add it just once to a single file that is included in every page.

That tiny bit of script provides Google Analytics with a huge amount of information about the people viewing your site, including where they are coming from, what they are looking at, and what technology they are using. All this is displayed in dozens of reports with

fancy charts and tables, but there are a few key figures you'll want to look out for.

You'll want to know the total number of visits and pages seen, but it is the "absolute unique visitors" and "unique page views" figures that you should pay most attention to. Your best friend might open up your site every day and look at dozens of pages, but they would only be counted as one unique visitor and the pages visited only counted once. The "bounce rate" is also important because it is an indicator of the visit quality—it's the percentage of single-page visits and so a high figure will mean that a large proportion of the people who come to your site find that the content is not relevant to them.

If you go into the content reports you'll be able to see which are the most popular pages and which ones get no traffic at all. The "in-page analytics" provides an image of your web page

with an overlay of how popular particular links are—this could illustrate that the clearest links near the top of the page attract the most attention, with the less obvious sections getting overlooked.

The traffic sources overview will tell you how people are getting to your site, which will either be directly from people typing in the URL, through referring sites, or from search engines. Check here to see how effective your marketing campaigns have been—how much traffic are you getting from adverts and links on external sites? What search engine keywords are leading people to your site? Is your social media activity leading to an increase in traffic?

If you want to get a little more advanced with your analysis, you can start setting goals. These are a way of measuring how well your site meets your business objectives and are particularly important for ecommerce websites.

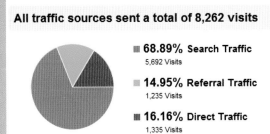

The Google Analytics traffic sources overview monitors where your visitors are coming from, so you can check the effectiveness of external sources.

Other traffic monitoring services are available, such as 1&1 SiteAnalytics.

For example, you might want to set the goal as the "payment confirmed" page. If you found that you were attracting loads of visits to your site but very few were "converted" into a sale, you'll want to investigate why that might be the case.

You can set up "funnels," which includes the path you expect your visitors to take to reach the goal, such as looking at the product list, adding to the shopping cart, selecting delivery options, and adding payment details. You can use this to see whether people are giving up at any particular step in the process, which might highlight changes you need to make.

Google Analytics can provide you with a huge amount of information about your website, but the most important thing is to keep an eye on trends over time. If traffic is increasing every month, you'll know that you are doing something right. If it is going nowhere, or even falling, you know you need to take action.

Reports can be scheduled, so you or your clients can be sent regular updates on your website's performance.

Your traffic stats will be incredibly useful for helping you develop your website once it has launched, so be sure to pay close attention to what they are telling you. They will help you learn what works and what doesn't, that in turn will help you build other sites in the future.

Don't try to compare traffic stats between different monitoring services, because they all count traffic in different ways. Google Analytics is likely to show much lower traffic than the services often offered by hosting companies, for example, which usually count all requests made to the server rather than actual views in a web browser. There will be pros and cons to each approach, but the important thing is to focus on the trends rather than the totals.

Chapter 11
Promote Your Website

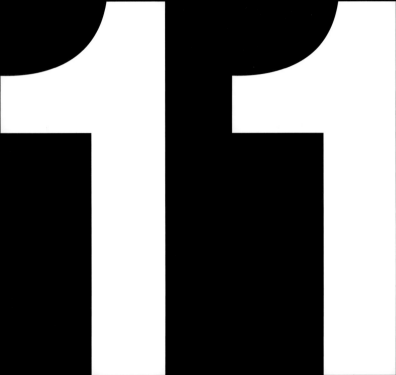

Why promotion is essential

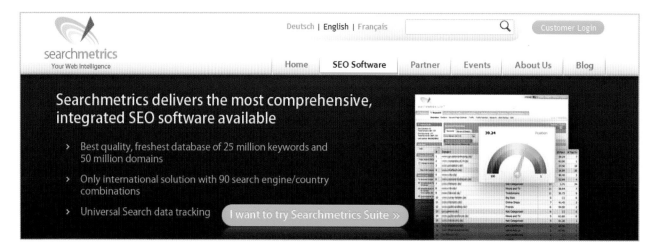

Having a great-looking website with engaging content is no good if nobody knows it is there. Even the most average of websites can attract thousands of visitors if it gets its marketing right.

The trouble is that marketing is possibly the most difficult aspect of website design and management, particularly if you are starting from scratch. The old adage "if you build it, they will come" is rarely true and you will have to put a considerable amount of time and effort into promoting your website if you want it to succeed.

You will be off to a good start if you have followed the advice offered already. Once your site is established, you'll be relying on Google to bring you much of your traffic, and search engines love clean, well-structured, standards-compliant code as well as clear and relevant content.

Take some time to plan how you are going let the world know about your website when it launches. There are many simple and free methods to promote your site, such as using social media sites like Facebook, Twitter, and LinkedIn, and submitting to free directories. You need to get links to your site in as many places as possible.

Although you can promote your site pretty well without spending a penny, it is often worth paying for targeted marketing, both online and offline.

Whatever you do, don't do nothing. And when your site is up and running, don't just sit back and admire your work—you'll need to keep promoting your site to keep the people coming.

There are software packages to help you identify how you can best optimize your pages and promote your site. Check out the comprehensive but pricey Searchmetrics Suite at www.searchmetrics.com or Traffic Travis at www.traffictravis.com, which also has a free version available.

Home

Keyword Tools

Search Engine
Tools

PPC Analysis

Page Analysis

SEO Analysis

Keyword Tools

▸ Keyword Finder
▸ Keyword Sorter

Search Engine Tools

▸ Position / Ranking
▸ Top sites for keywords
▸ Backlinks to site
▸ Project Report

PPC Analysis

▸ Keywords / Details
▸ Top sites for keywords
▸ Most popular keywords
▸ Websites keyword list

Be search-engine friendly

Google Insights for Search lets you compare search patterns across specific regions and categories to help you identify the keywords you need to target: www.google.com/insights/search/#.

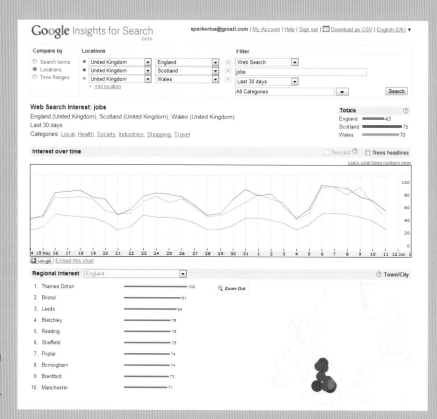

If your website is going to be successful, you are going to have to get friendly with the search engines. Nobody knows *exactly* what search engines want from your pages to give them a good ranking, and the methods they use are always being tweaked, so what can you do to ingratiate yourself with Google?

The best approach is simply to build a good website with relevant content. Trying to "trick" Google into giving you a better ranking could end in tears, because the search engine giant has got very good at spotting all the underhand methods used over the years.

Google will favor well-structured and standards-compliant code, weighting relevance of your content to the users search terms by taking into consideration what is represented in the HTML mark-up, for example, heading tags and paragraphs. The way you structure your content will reflect how search engines are able to determine its relevance.

Remember that search engines also index images and video content. Marking these elements with alternate text and relevant headings can also serve to help drive traffic.

Clear and descriptive page titles—the text contained in the <title> tags, which is shown on your browser tab—are helpful for people navigating your pages, but they are also used when your pages are listed in search engines.

You should remember that these titles are what the end-user sees in their search results, so it is important not to just fill the title element with keywords relevant to your content, but to accurately and concisely—note that Google will only display the first sixty-six characters of your title—describe what they can expect to get when they visit your page. Search engine crawlers will also take a look at all the content on your page and see how often particular words or phrases appear compared to the total number of words on the page. So, if your website is all about eco-friendly light bulbs, you want to make sure you include

Word clouds can also be a useful way to assess your content—the larger the text, the more frequently the word appears. This is a cloud created from the homepage of the 2012 London Olympics website using wordle.net.

keywords like "light bulbs," "energy saving," and "lighting" in your content.

Keyword density was once a major factor in how search engines ranked pages, but it is far less important now. This is because people began to stuff too many keywords into their text in a bid to artificially boost their position, so don't go overboard with your keywords or you could end up being penalized—anything

over 5% density for a particular word or phrase might be considered "spamming." You can check keyword density using online tools like www.seobay.com/tools/keyword-density-checker.

How quickly your page downloads might also be a factor considered by search engines, so be as efficient as possible. Check the ratio of text to HTML because the more actual content

there is compared to code the better—aim for anything more than 20%. Optimize images, keep scripts and styles in separate files, and don't try to jam too much content onto one page; the search engine crawlers will give up reading if it is too long, so any useful content at the foot of the page might be missed.

Metadata: Dead and buried?

Once upon a time, it was all about the meta tags—content that provides information about your page but is not shown to your visitors. But systematic abuse by people trying to artificially boost their search rankings means that they have become much less important.

It is still good to get metadata right though, particularly the meta descriptions that will often be shown in your search engine listings. Each page should have a unique meta description that accurately describes the page, but if you have a large site and that is not practical, focus on the main pages. Meta descriptions should be between around seventy to 160 characters, be readable, and highlight factual information about the content. The clearer your description is, the more likely people are to follow the link.

If you are using a content management system like WordPress, meta descriptions can be automatically generated to include key details, and you can use plug-ins to manually change the descriptions when editing pages.

It is thought that the meta keywords element is largely ignored now, but adding it will do you no harm. Other meta elements include language and author, and there are those that identify technical details about your page, but they should not affect your rankings. Some search engines might take geo meta tags into consideration to highlight place names, regions, or even

The All in One SEO Pack plug-in for WordPress makes optimizing pages a breeze: wordpress.org/extend/plugins/all-in-one-seo-pack.

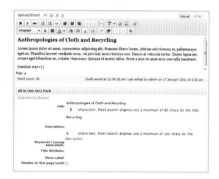

Geo sitemaps can also be created and submitted to Google using tools like GeoSitemapGenerator.com. This is particularly useful if your business operates at many different locations.

The specifications of microformats like hCard can be found at microformats.org.

coordinates. This is particularly relevant for mobile users using location-based services, like finding the nearest store.

The meta robots element can be useful, because you can give instructions to search engine crawlers when they come to your page—like telling them whether to index your page, archive a cached version, or follow links from the page—but using a robots.txt file is a more reliable method.

Many site owners are now using microformats or RDF (Resource Description Framework) to convey metadata in web pages, tagging content to help search engines understand what they are looking at. Although it is unclear how search engines are using these elements and what effect, if any, they have on the ranking of your pages, it could become an increasingly important way of marking up your content.

The most common microformat used on web pages is the hCard, which is used to highlight contact information like name, address, and phone number. It is also worth investigating hCalendar and other "rich snippets"—see googlewebmastercentral.blogspot.com/2009/05/introducing-rich-snippets.html.

Get your pages indexed

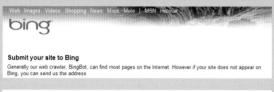

Help search engines index your site by submitting a URL to www.bing.com/webmaster/SubmitSitePage.aspx and www.google.com/addurl.

Create an XML sitemap for your website to submit to Google, Bing, and other search engines with: www.xml-sitemaps.com.

Google Webmaster Tools provides lots of data about your search engine performance and will highlight any issues with your pages. You can see how Google crawls and indexes your site, how many people found your site in the search results, and who is linking to you. You can then use this information to optimize your pages further.

As long as your site is linked from a page somewhere on the web, search engine spiders should find and index your site soon enough, but there is no harm in giving them a helping hand to make sure that all your pages are indexed accurately.

You can submit a URL address to Google at www.google.com/addurl and to Microsoft's Bing at www.bing.com/webmaster/SubmitSitePage.aspx.

You should have a sitemap on your site so that search engines can easily crawl and index your pages accordingly, but you should also submit XML sitemaps to Google. To do this, you need to sign up to Google Webmaster Tools at www.google.com/webmasters.

Creating an XML sitemap is simple—all you need is a normal text editor like Notepad, and you just list all the URLs of your pages with the appropriate tags that search engines will read and recognize. For more information on how to create sitemaps see www.sitemaps.org, but the easiest way is to use online services like www.xml-sitemaps.com or install the appropriate plug-in for your content management system.

Once created, your sitemap needs to be copied to your web space and then submitted using Google Webmaster Tools. If you have many pages, it is worth creating and submitting multiple sitemaps for different themes, although make sure they all have different names and don't repeat the same links. If your site changes,

be sure to update the relevant sitemaps and resubmit them.

There might also be content that you don't want search engines to index. For example, you might have copyrighted images that you don't want to appear on an image search. You can create exclusions using a robots.txt file, which can be generated using Webmaster Tools. This file needs to sit in your top-level web directory and then search robots will check it before indexing your pages.

Build links
to your pages

Check who is linking to your site
using tools like Yahoo's Site Explorer
(siteexplorer.search.yahoo.com).

PRWeb will distribute articles
and press releases for you to
improve search engine listings.

Widgets like www.addthis.com
will add "sharing" buttons to
your website making it easy
for people to link to you via
social media.

Although Google will appreciate your clean code and keyword-rich content, what it really wants is links to your pages. The logic goes that if lots of people are linking to you, then your content must be relevant and useful. Not all links are treated equally, though—a link on a high-ranking site will give your site more of a boost than a link on an obscure blog.

Your first targets are the social media sites, like Facebook, Twitter, and LinkedIn. You will have posted a link to your site on your profiles and updates, of course, but you should also make it easy for others to share links with friends, followers, and connections. There are "widgets" available that add share buttons to your pages, such as www.addthis.com, sharethis.com, and www.addtoany.com.

Look at relevant blogs and forums that discuss your field and suggest your site where appropriate, or simply add it to your signature. Listing on directories will help, but also contact other websites to ask if they would consider adding a link to your pages. Try to add a link to your site wherever you can—you could even add your site to the appropriate Wikipedia entries.

Write articles and press releases that include a link to your pages and then submit them to a news site or distribution service like www.prweb.com or www.pressking.com. You might need to pay for this, but your news could reach thousands of people through newsfeeds and search engine listings.

The key is to make sure that anywhere that lists your site is relevant—if you bombard dozens of sites indiscriminately, you will just annoy people and could even be penalized on Google. Don't be sucked into too many reciprocal link arrangements, as these could be seen as an attempt to artificially boost your ranking, and you could be penalized accordingly.

Just like the internal links on your website, it will help if external links to your pages have meaningful anchor text. Rather than a "click here" or "this site," you'd want the link to say "second-hand clothes" if it took people to a page selling second-hand clothes. You might not always be able to control this, and any link back to your site is welcome, but the more relevant the link text, the better.

You can invest in the services of an expert, but take care with companies that offer search engine optimization, especially if they promise top rankings in double-quick time. There are many unscrupulous providers that might charge a lot for doing little more than you could easily do yourself. Even worse, they may use tactics that could see your site blacklisted.

That's not to say that they are all bad. What they should be doing is advising you on the content of your pages and adding your links to accurate, relevant, and keyword-heavy articles and posts on reputable websites. What is reputable or relevant is often a matter of judgment, but make sure you are happy with what they're writing and where they're posting it. A good link-building campaign that runs over a number of months can have a huge impact on your search engine rankings.

Get listed in directories

Google Places even provides a dashboard to show you where and when your entry is being displayed, so you can see just how effective your listing is. See www.google.com/places.

Google Places works particularly well for local businesses that have a bricks-and-mortar side, especially if you can encourage positive reviews!

Get Listed checks your listing with the major local search directories and suggests where else you can list your business: getlisted.org.

Although the value of online directories has been on the decline for some time, it is still worth taking some simple steps to get yourself listed, particularly for location-based searches. If you want your business to show up on Google Maps, then you need to have a free listing on Google Places. You can add your business areas, contact details, business hours, payment details, and more, and customers have the chance to rate and review your services. Your entry will also be indexed by Google's search engine and will often appear at the top of the page for location-based search queries.

Perhaps the most well-known of all web directories is Yahoo! (dir.yahoo.com), where all sites are reviewed by real people before being listed. You can submit your site for free by following the "Suggest a Site" link on the

relevant category page in the directory, but don't hold your breath for a listing.

There is a price to pay for jumping to the front of the queue and getting listed, and that is $299 with a recurring annual fee, but be aware that because each submission will be given the once-over by humans, you are not guaranteed the description or placement you want.

Yahoo! also offers a local listings service similar to Google Places that is free, although you can pay for an enhanced entry: zlistings.local.yahoo.com.

Another directory you should look to get on is the Open Directory Project (dmoz.org). Again, real people will review any sites you submit, but it is a multilingual open-content

project that uses volunteer editors. Because it is not commercial, you can't pay to get considered more quickly. It might take weeks before your submission is even looked at and longer still before your site is actually listed—if you are lucky to get it listed at all.

There are many other local or industry-specific directories, so do a bit of research to see what might be suitable. Anything that is relevant and free is worth signing up for, even if it only gives a minor boost to your search ranking. Take care with directories that require payment—test out how they perform in Google by taking some relevant keywords and locations and seeing if any competing listings from the directory appear near the top of list. If they do, it might be worth making the investment.

Advertise with Google AdWords

Google's search results page includes adverts at the top of the page and in the right column.

Google AdWords provides a comprehensive control panel to help you monitor and manage your campaigns, so you can play around with what works and what does not.

Other advertising services are available, including Microsoft's AdCenter (adcenter.microsoft.com) and Yahoo! Advertising Solutions (advertisingcentral.yahoo.com).

If you are prepared to pay for a bit of advertising, a good place to start is Google AdWords. This lets you create simple text adverts that are displayed on Google search result pages and across a network of partner sites. These ads will only appear when people are looking for something relevant to your business.

How much it costs depends on your location and how many customers you are trying to reach, but the beauty of AdWords is that you only pay when someone actually clicks on your link and you can control how much you spend from day to day.

Where and when your adverts appear will depend on what keywords you select and how much competition there is for those keywords. The more you are prepared to bid for each click, the more likely your advert will appear. If your bid is the highest, your advert will be shown at the top of the list.

Google provides lots of assistance to help you choose relevant keywords and set your budgets, although you will stand a much better chance at getting your advert shown if you are targeting a niche audience. You might not get very far if you bid a small amount for the phrase "digital cameras" because the competition will be steep, but if you have a specific product like "rubber chickens" you might have more luck.

Create a Facebook page

Facebook offers a range of social plug-ins for your site (developers. facebook.com/docs/plugins).

The rise of Facebook has been phenomenal, and with more than 600 million users worldwide, businesses are increasingly taking the opportunity to reach out to this huge audience. Every business or organization, big or small, should have its own Facebook public profile. It might not be hugely effective for everyone, but it's free and only takes a few minutes to set up, so there is no excuse.

A Facebook public profile is similar to creating a personal profile, but rather than connecting with friends, anyone can "Like" your page and follow what you are doing. You can then communicate with those people by posting updates, images, and, of course, links back to your site.

Search engines will index your Facebook public profile, giving your site more exposure and improving your page ranking. But perhaps the most powerful feature is that you can publish posts to your fans' newsfeeds so that they appear on their personal pages, which means you can reach whole new audience.

Check out Facebook's advertising service at www. facebook.com/advertising.

Insights shows you Facebook activity associated with your profile and your website: www.facebook.com/insights.

Encourage people to visit your Facebook page by placing an obvious link to your profile on your web pages and emails. Also take advantage of your personal profile and share the link with your friends.

To make the most of Facebook, you have to work hard at it. Post regular updates and make sure you link back to your site, enticing people with special offers or details about exciting new products. Think about the time you post too: when is your audience most likely to be online? Try tracking what you do

and how effective it has been each time, so you can perfect the art of posting.

If you want to reach further beyond your friends and fans, Facebook also offers an advertising service. Simple adverts appear in the right-hand column of Facebook pages and can be targeted to your chosen audience by location, age, and interests. You can set a daily budget you are comfortable with, although the more you pay the more your advert will appear. See www.facebook. com/advertising.

Make the most of Twitter

Tools like Tweetburner can help you shorten your URLs, then share and track them so you can tell how well you're promoting your site.

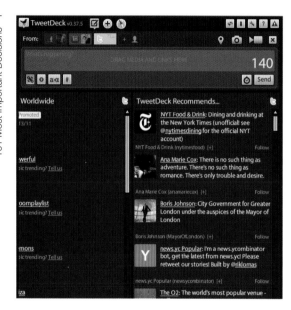

Tweetdeck makes it easy to manage your tweets wherever are, and you can link up with your Facebook and LinkedIn profiles so you might only need to post once to be seen across all sites. See www.tweetdeck.com.

It's often hard to believe that Twitter's micro-blogging service (www.twitter.com) has become so popular, but there is no doubt that it has become a powerful influence on societies across the world.

Twitter's strength is its simplicity and inclusivity. It's easy to set up and then you simply post very short updates—a maximum of 140 characters—in the hope that people will "follow" you to see what you have to say. You can, of course, follow other people and join in discussions about a myriad of topics from the serious to the banal.

Twitter has proven to be an effective marketing tool, because the audience you could potentially reach is huge. You will find that if you follow someone, they will often follow you back.

Then others will follow you just because they can see their contacts following you and so it goes on. Pretty soon you could have thousands of people receiving your small pearls of wisdom on their PCs or mobile devices.

You can't just get away with writing nonsense all the time, though, if you want to promote your website. You need to post something relevant and potentially useful to your followers, like a new product release or special offer. If you are lucky and they find it interesting, they might "retweet" your message to all their followers, who then might pass it on to theirs, and so on. If you have sensibly provided a link back to your site, you might get some new visitors as a result of your tweets.

Make sure you have a link to your Twitter account on your website and highlight it on your Facebook and LinkedIn page. You can also add buttons to your site that allow people to easily share your pages with others.

Although Twitter is simple to use, it can be hard to get into the habit of regularly tweeting interesting snippets, but the more you use it, the more effective it will be. Don't just use it for promoting your site—people will be much more likely to pay attention to your tweets if they are not all about marketing. Keep it personal and pass on details of other useful articles you have seen and join in discussions about things that are relevant to your business. You can also use it to get views and advice from your followers.

Create a newsfeed

Feedity can turn your
content into an RSS feed:
www.feedity.com.

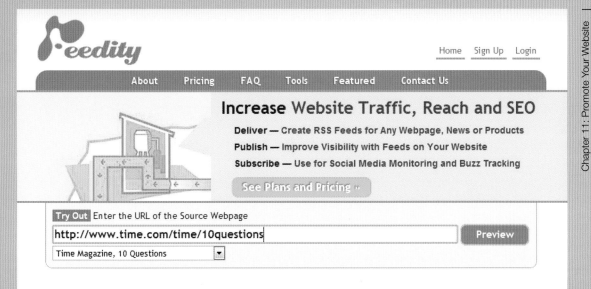

If you have regularly changing content—like a blog or news page—you should consider syndicating it as a feed to whomever wants it. This can be done using the RSS format (Rich Site Summary, but often known as Really Simple Syndication).

RSS files are simply XML formatted plain text, where elements like the title, description, and link are tagged accordingly. Your site's visitors could then subscribe to your RSS feed and view your news using a feed reader or aggregator. They could even take your feed and display your news on their site.

Your feed needs to be saved as an XML file in your web directory, and then you need to provide a button or link for people to subscribe to your feed. All news items should have a link back to your pages, so the more people

subscribe to your feed, the more likely you are to get people returning to your site.

Although you can create your RSS file manually using a text editor, updating it could become tiresome. Most content management systems will have a plug-in that generates an RSS feed automatically from your blog or news pages, or you can develop your own dynamic RSS generator.

Services like Feedity can take the content from any page and turn it into an RSS feed and update it when new content is added: www.feedity.com.

Once you have a feed you should add it to Google's FeedBurner (feedburner.google. com). This service lets you analyze, optimize, and publicize your feed using a range of tools.

You can download feed icons for free to help people subscribe to your RSS feed.

Get on YouTube

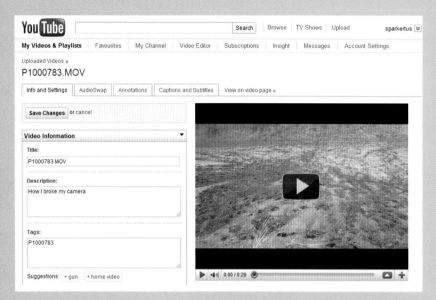

Posting an interesting or entertaining video on YouTube is a good way to reach out to new audiences for your website.

YouTube is the number one place to go for video content on the web, with millions of people across the world visiting the site every day. Uploading your own videos and tapping in to this huge audience can be a great way to promote your site.

First you need to record your movies. You don't need particularly high-tech equipment—a decent webcam or digital camera will do the trick—and it doesn't need to have slick production and editing either. In fact, a "home-movie" feel could give it that personal touch, which might make it more engaging.

Your videos don't need to be TV-style commercials that just tell people how wonderful you are. A product demonstration might work better, but something that offers genuinely useful advice would be even more effective.

For example, if your site sells model airplanes, an instructional video on "how to paint your models like an expert" would be more popular than a commercial shouting about how you have the cheapest prices on the web.

If you were feeling particularly confident, you could go for the comedy angle in the hope that people would find it so hilarious that they passed it on to all their friends. It's easy to get this wrong, of course, and you might find that your attempts at humor still get circulated just because they are so bad. They say that all publicity is good publicity, but just remember that anyone can comment on your videos and what they say might not be too nice.

The key point is that the more people find your movie interesting or entertaining, the more likely they are to share it. Remember

that you want people to come to your site after seeing your wonderful work, so make sure you show or mention your website address.

Adding your movie to YouTube is simple. Just follow the "Upload" link, select the file you want to use from your computer, and then wait for it to appear. A wide variety of formats is accepted and the videos can be up to 2GB in size and fifteen minutes in length.

Then comes the search engine optimization, which works in a similar way to optimizing your web pages. You provide a description of the video and tags that include the keywords most relevant to your video and likely to be searched for.

World Guitars provides demonstrations, interviews, and testimonials using YouTube videos embedded in its pages: www.worldguitars.co.uk.

Make sure that your video is made public so people are able to find it in their video search results, but you'll also be given a URL that you can share. Just like your website, the more links you have to your video, the more likely it is to appear in searches, so put links to your video wherever you can. Share the video on all the usual social media channels to get maximum exposure—you can even connect your YouTube account to Facebook, Twitter, and so on, so that your uploads are automatically added to your profiles.

Your movies don't have to be all about promoting your website; they can give your site great content too. You will get a code snippet that lets you embed your video in your webpage so people can see your masterpiece without leaving your site.

To really make the most of YouTube you need to build up an audience and continue to give them what they want to see. People will be able to subscribe to your channel to always get any future videos you produce, and you can use YouTube to post messages to your subscribers.

MiniWarGaming at www.youtube.com/user/miniwargaming provides a huge range of content for table-top enthusiasts and performs well for video searches on the relevant keywords. This is bound to drive people to their website and to their stores.

Create an email newsletter

One of the most effective ways to keep in touch with your users is by email, sending them regular updates on what is happening on your site. This could be to let people know about new products or special offers or just to share useful news and information.

To give your missives greater impact, you can create HTML emails that include your site's branding and links to entice readers back to your site. Unfortunately, designing HTML emails is not always straightforward, because most email clients don't read HTML in the same way as your web browser. To make things even harder, all email clients see things differently—so what looks fine in Outlook, for example, might look very different in Gmail.

Designing for email means turning your back on current best practice and returning to the bad old days. Layouts are usually created using tables and any styles often need to be applied to every element rather than specified only once. Anything you create then needs be tested across as many email clients as possible, and you might find yourself pulling your hair out until you get it right.

The next challenge is creating an email that doesn't get blocked because it looks too much like spam. Almost all email clients, internet service providers, and large organizations will have some kind of anti-spam protection, but how it is applied might be very different for each one. A single innocent word like "sex" could mean your email goes straight to the junk bin.

Thankfully, there are services available that make email marketing so much easier. MailChimp (www.mailchimp.com) is one of the best and offers bags of advice on how to create the perfect email newsletter. It's easy to manage your subscribers and create your campaigns all through your web browser. The Inbox Inspector tool even allows you to check your campaigns across all major email clients and spam filters before you press the button to send. It's free if you have a small subscriber list and don't use all of the features on offer, otherwise monthly plans and pay-as-you-go packages are available.

Keep the content of any email newsletters and promotions brief and remember that people might be viewing them on a small screen. Newsletters don't have to be all about marketing, but the goal should always be to get people to follow links back to your site. Text should be limited to teasers, and images should highlight your key messages. You can use images for text to give them more impact and make things more consistent for all viewers, but note that many email clients will not download images by default. Personalization can be a nice touch to make your messages look more than generic bulk-emails.

Once you have sent your email, you should monitor how effective it has been. Campaign Monitor and MailChimp show you exactly who has opened your email and what links they have followed, and you can then follow up with those who have shown an interest. Take note of what is popular and what is not, so you can make your next newsletter even better.

MailChimp is an excellent resource. It offers advice and helps you create, share, and distribute your newsletter, as well as tracking the results.

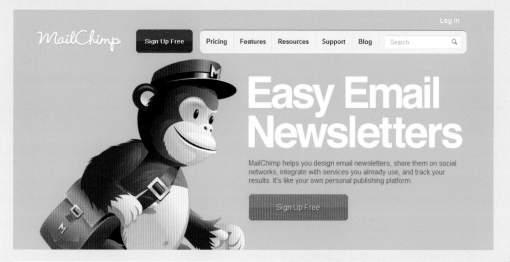

The Law

Both MailChimp and Campaign Monitor follow U.S. anti-spam legislation, which is very strict on who you can send your messages to and what they contain. It insists that everyone on your mailing list has explicitly agreed that you can send them email communications, so people have to "opt in" to receive your newsletters.

The equivalent European Directive isn't quite so tough, and you can include emails from existing customers whose addresses you have obtained "in the course of a sale or negotiations for the sale," as long as you will be marketing similar products and services to them. In this case, you must give people the opportunity to easily "opt out" when you collect their details and in any subsequent communications.

Be sure to check the latest legislation in your region and take care when adding addresses to your subscriber database—never use bought-in mailing lists or trawl the web for addresses—otherwise your unsolicited emails may well be labeled as spam, and you could be blacklisted.

Wherever you are and whatever service you are using, always provide your name and contact details on your messages and give people a clear way of unsubscribing should they wish to.

If designing an email newsletter from scratch sounds too much like hard work, Campaign Monitor offers some excellent free templates from top designers: www.campaignmonitor.com/templates.

Monitor the performance of your email newsletter.

Promote your site offline

Online services such as inkd.com offer great flyer templates for you to customize and print.

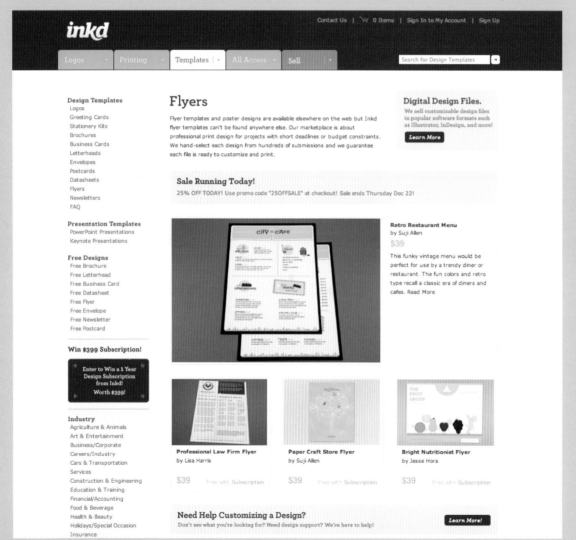

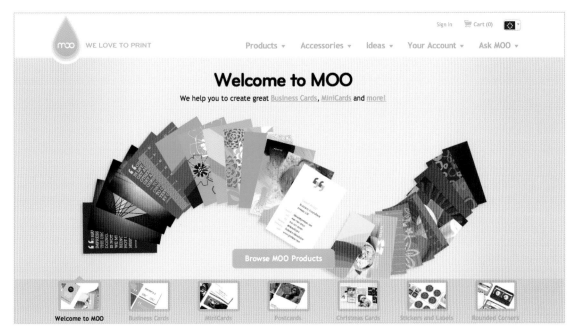

Your promotion activity does not have to be limited to the online world; traditional marketing can be just as effective.

If your business has a local focus, targeting local newspapers and circulars can be an effective way of leading people to your website or giving you a call. Trade or special interest publications are also worth looking at—advertise where your audience is likely to be looking.

Prices will vary widely depending on where you are and how large the circulation is, but weigh up how many leads you would need to get from the ads to cover the costs. Make your ads look professional and offer incentives like special offers for readers to help lure people to your site.

Get your web address out there wherever you can—maybe a bumper sticker on your car or a sign outside your home or office. Consider distributing flyers at relevant locations and link up with other local businesses offering related products and services. For example, if you provide garden landscaping services, get a local builder to pass on your business card to his clients.

Check out your local business enterprise center and see if there are any events you can go along to where you might meet potential clients. "Business breakfast" gatherings at 7 a.m. aren't everyone's idea of fun, but this kind of networking can be very effective if you manage to get yourself in with the local business community.

Go the traditional route—the easy way. There are plenty of sites that offer free business card templates or flyer designs for you to download and customize, such as moo.com.

References

Glossary

Accessibility: Making websites usable by people of all abilities, including those with visual impairments and other disabilities.

Adaptive layout: A variation of fluid web page layouts, where different layouts are presented for different media, such as mobile phone, tablet, and high-resolution screens.

Anchor text: The visible text that you click on through a hyperlink.

Asp.NET: Web application framework developed by Microsoft used to build dynamic websites.

Back-end: Part of the website not visible to regular users, including admin functions, databases, and applications.

Breadcrumb: Navigation aid that shows the path to the current web page, usually found at the top of the content.

Browser: Software program used to view websites, such as Internet Explorer, Mozilla Firefox, or Google Chrome.

Cascading Style Sheets (CSS): Language used to define presentational aspects of a website, usually in a separate document from the HTML files.

Client-side: Operations that are carried out in the viewer's browser, rather than on the web server.

Content Management System (CMS): Web-based tool used to edit and manage the content of a website, often making it easier for those that have limited technical skills to make amendments.

Domain: The name used to identify a particular website address, such as www.mydomain.com.

Domain Name System (DNS): Naming system for any resource connected to the Internet, allowing domain names to be associated with particular web servers and websites.

Favicon: Small customizable icon displayed in the address bar and tabs on most web browsers.

Fixed width: Web page layout that has a set width, so that it stays the same size whatever the screen resolution. Often used to ensure greater control of how a website looks across all browsers and platforms.

Fluid layout: Also know as a "liquid layout," this is a web page layout that will change depending on the width of the browser. This is used to make the most of the space, as the page will expand to fill the whole screen.

Fold: From the newspaper term "above the fold" that describes the visible part of the page on the newsstands. The fold is the point at which you will need to scroll down to view the rest of the content on a web page, but this will be different for different users.

Front-end (or user interface): The part of the website visible to regular visitors to a website.

.htaccess: File used to configure Apache web servers, mainly used to handle compression, caching, URL writing, and redirects.

HTML: Hyper Text Markup Language, the language used to write web pages, using a variety of specified "tags" attached to content.

iFrame (or inline frame): Used to display content from a different website within a web page.

Inline style: CSS that is written on the web page, directly around the element it affects, rather than in a separate style sheet.

Javascript: Popular scripting language used to write functions to be used on web pages. Common uses are for form validation and dynamic visual effects.

jQuery: Free, open-source JavaScript library that lets people create complex dynamic effects without the need for advanced technical skills.

Markup: The code used to create a web page.

Metadata: Data on a web page that contains information that is not visible to the visitor.

Navigation: Means used to allow visitors to find their way around a website using menus, breadcrumbs, and the links on a web page.

Open Source: Software code that is made available to the general public, often developed by teams of volunteers and usually free of charge.

Permalink: Short for "permanent link," it is the permanent URL given to a blog post to make sure people can always bookmark or share the post, wherever it might appear on the website. Permalinks are usually rewritten to offer easy-to-read and search-engine friendly addresses.

PHP (or PHP: Hypertext Preprocessor): Popular server-side scripting language used for developing dynamic web pages. Usually used on Unix/Linux server platforms, and often used in association with MySQL databases.

Plug-in: Third-party code that extends the functionality of a website, often through a Content Management System. Also refers to add-ons for web browsers like Firefox.

Property: Term used in CSS that is a property name followed with a value to define how an element should be displayed on a web page, such as "padding:0."

Pseudo-element: Used in CSS to add a special effect to certain selectors, such as "a:hover."

RSS (Really Simple Syndication or RDF Site Summary): Format used to allow you to syndicate web content as a newsfeed. Feeds can be read with software called an "RSS reader" or "aggregator."

Script: Usually refers to code that controls dynamic elements of a website, using languages like JavaScript.

Selector: In CSS, the selector specifies which item on the web page a style is applied to.

Semantic Markup: Code that is written to offer context to what the content is for or about, making it easier for humans and machines to understand the information. For example, all headings will have heading tags and all elements will have names that describe what they are rather than what they look like.

Server-side: Scripts that are run on the web server, rather than in the browser.

Sitemap: Page that lists the content available on a website, used to help navigation. XML sitemaps can also be submitted to search engines to ensure that all pages are indexed.

Standards-compliant: Adhering to the web standards proposed by the World Wide Web Consortium (W3C) and so more likely to have better interoperability between different platforms and browsers.

SVG (Scalable Vector Graphics): XML-based format used for both static and animated vector graphics. Although it is a standard specified by the W3C and supported by most browsers, it is not commonly used.

Tag: In HTML, each element has a start tag and end tag wrapped around content, such as "<h1>My website</h1>."

Template: A set of files that can be customized to use with different websites and employ a consistent design across all pages. Also known as themes, particularly in connection with Content Management Systems.

URL (Uniform Resource Locator): A web page's address that can used to find its location on the internet.

Usability: How easy a website is to use. The goal is to make all web pages clear and intuitive to all visitors, without them needing to think too hard or ask for help.

Validation: Checking that web pages are error-free and conform to the W3C specifications. Valid code is more likely to work consistently across all browsers and platforms.

Web server: Computer hardware or software that is used to host a website and deliver web pages over a network.

XHTML (Extensible Hypertext Markup Language): Strict version of HTML rewritten to follow XML rules. Writing in XHTML will mean that your code is more likely to work across all platforms.

XML (Extensible Markup Language): Textual data format that defines a set of rules for writing other markup languages.

Index

References
Index

The Web Designer's
101 Most Important Decisions

Acknowledgments

A massive thank you to James Dickie,
the person I turn to whenever I have a tricky
web design problem to sort out. I've learnt
more from him than I could from any book or
website and he helped make sure that I was
not writing complete nonsense.

Thanks also to Dave Wilby for his valuable
contribution, Sean McManus for getting me
started, and Kim Gilmour for all her advice
and encouragement.

I must also thank my wife Claire and my family
for their support, without which I would never
have got it all finished.